POLARIZATION AROUND THE CHARACTER OF ‘ALĪ IBN ABĪ ṬĀLIB (A.S.)

MURTAḌĀ MUṬAHHARĪ

English translation
First edition 1981/1401
Second edition 1985/1405

Translated from the Persian
Jādhibah wa dāfi'ah-e 'Alī 'alayhi 's-salām
Tehran, 1349 Sh./ 1391 A. H.

Translated and Published by:
World Organization for Islamic Services,
P. O. Box No. 11365 - 1545,
Tehran - IRAN

In the Name of Allāh,
The All-compassionate, The All-merciful

Praise belongs to Allāh, the Lord of all being,
the All-compassionate; the All-merciful;
the Master of the Day of Judgement;
Thee only, we serve, and to Thee alone we pray
for succour;
Guide us in the straight path;
the path of those whom Thou hast blessed,
not of those against whom Thou art wrathful,
nor of those who are astray.

* * * * *

O Allāh! send your blessings to the head of
your messengers and the last of
your prophets,
Muḥammad and his pure and cleansed progeny.
Also send your blessings to all your
prophets and envoys.

بِسْمِ اللهِ الرَّحْمٰنِ الرَّحِيمِ ﴿١﴾
اَلْحَمْدُ لِلّٰهِ رَبِّ الْعٰلَمِيْنَ ﴿٢﴾ الرَّحْمٰنِ الرَّحِيْمِ ﴿٣﴾
مٰلِكِ يَوْمِ الدِّيْنِ ﴿٤﴾ إِيَّاكَ نَعْبُدُ وَإِيَّاكَ نَسْتَعِيْنُ ﴿٥﴾
اِهْدِنَا الصِّرَاطَ الْمُسْتَقِيْمَ ﴿٦﴾ صِرَاطَ الَّذِيْنَ أَنْعَمْتَ
عَلَيْهِمْ غَيْرِ الْمَغْضُوْبِ عَلَيْهِمْ وَلَا الضَّآلِّيْنَ ﴿٧﴾

اَللّٰهُمَّ صَلِّ عَلٰى
سَيِّدِ رُسُلِكَ وَ خٰاتَمِ اَنْبِيٰائِكَ
مُحَمَّدٍ وَاٰلِهِ الطَّيِّبِيْنَ الطّٰاهِرِينَ
وَ صَلِّ عَلٰى جَمِيعِ الْأَنْبِيٰاءِ وَالْمُرْسَلِين

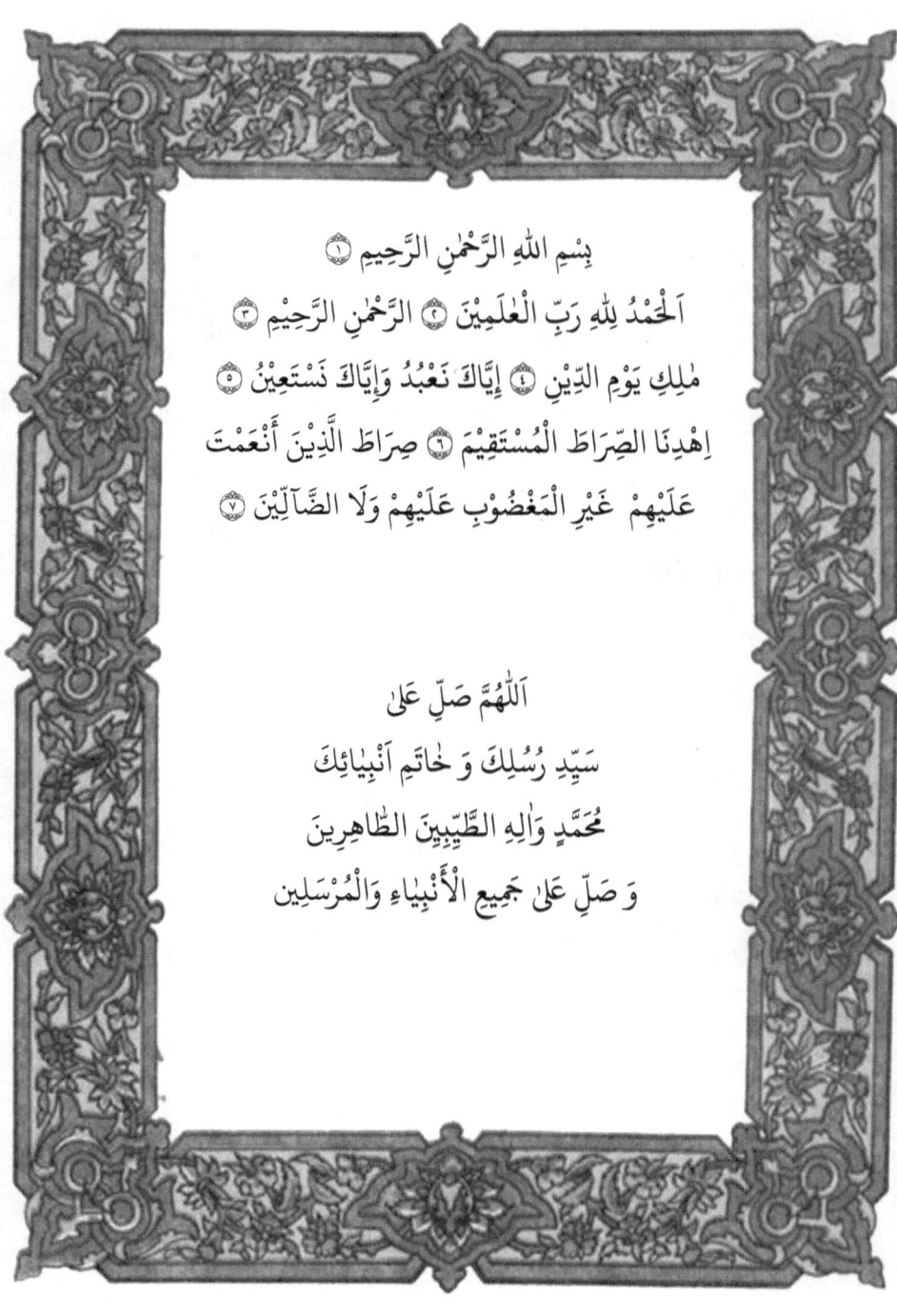

CONTENTS

TRANSLITERATION

Symbol	Transliteration	Symbol	Transliteration
ء	’	ل	l
ب	b	م	m
ت	t	ن	n
ث	th	و	w
ج	j	ه	h
ح	ḥ	ي	y
خ	kh	ة	ah
د	d		
ذ	dh	**Long Vowels**	
ر	r	ا	ā
ز	z	و	ū
س	s	ي	ī
ش	sh		
ص	ṣ	**Short Vowels**	
ض	ḍ	ـَ	a
ط	ṭ	ـُ	u
ظ	ẓ	ـِ	i
ع	‘		
غ	gh	**Persian Letters**	
ف	f	پ	p
ق	q	چ	ch
ك	k	ژ	zh
		گ	g

تصد ير

(جا ذبه و دافعه عليّ عليه السلام) او (قوّة الجذب وقوّة الدّفع في عليّ علببه السلام) اثر من أشهر اثار العلاّمة الكبير المغفور له (الشّيخ مرتضى مطّهرى) الكاتب الاسلاميّ الايرانيّ رحمه الله.

والمؤلّف نفسه قد فسرّ ما يقصده من هذا العنوان ضمن المقدّمة التّي وضعها وضمن البحوث التي تنا ولها بما اغنانا من اعادته في هذا التّصدير.

ولكنّنا يجب ان لا نغفل انّ قوّة جذب المحبّين والانصار، بل والمتفانين، في شخصيّةما، وتقا بلها قوّة الدّفع في تلك الشخصيّة - وهما التّعبيران اللّذ ان اختارهما المؤلّف - والّتي تخلق هذه الاخيرة لتلك الشصيّة خصوما واعداءا، بل وقتلة، ليستا بعاملين أوّليين في ايّة شخصيّة، بل انّهما تعبير ان يجمعان ما تناثر من العو امل والمؤثّرات الّتي ترتبط بتلك الشخصيّة.

فمنها العوامل الذّاتيّة (الداخليّة) التي تتواجد في تلك اشخصيّة والتي تخلق له المحبيّن والانصار او تخلق له المبغضين والاعداء، وتقا بلها العوامل الذاتيّة التي تتواجد في شخصيّات الانصار والاعداء أ نفسهم، والتي تتفا عل مع العوامل الاولى فتخلق منهم أنصارا أو اعداءا، ومنها الظروف والمؤثرات (العو امل) ألخارجيّة والتي توكّد فا عليّة تلك العوامل الذاتيّة، او تقف ما نعادون تأثيرها٠

والشخصيّة المبحوث عنها ان تجاوزت عصرها وزمانها، وكانت شخصيّة العصور والاجيال، فلا بدوان تتكوّن بالنسبة اليها ضمن هذه الحياة التاريخية الطويلة عوامل اضافيّة مساعدة او معارضة، ومن اهمّ هذه الأخيرة قائمة المحبيّن والمتفانين وشخصيّاتهم، وقائمة المناهضين والأعداء وشخصيّاتهم، والذين يزد ادون كلما امتدّ الزّمن، ومرّت القرون وتناسلت الأجيال.

والاهمّ من هذا كلّه أن لا نغفل عما اذا كان المبحوث عنه شخصيّة كأمير المؤمنين عليه السلام التّي امتزجت في ذاته المقدّسة أشرف الخصائص الانسانيّة باقوى المواهب الالهيّة، وامتزج في شيعته وفي خصومه الايما ن - كا قوى ما سكون — بالرّسالة الالهيّة بالايمان بالانسان وسموّ رسا لته في جانب، وامتزج التنكّر لرسالة السماء بالكفر بالانسانيّة والخروج عليها في جانب آخر.

اقول اننا ان وضعنا أمام أعيننا ما أشرنا اليه فاننا بهذا تتجسم امامنا عظمة الطّاقة والجهد الذي لابدّ وان يبذل ومدى سعة البحث وعمق الدّراسة الذي لابد وأن يهيّأ كي يكون العمل في مستوى

المسؤليّة، والنتيّجة منتهيا اليها من جميع جوانب مقدّماتها.

- ٢ -

هذا الكتاب كما ذكره العلامة المؤلف نفسه، رحمه الله كان في الأصل اربع محاضرات القاها بمناسبة ذكرى استشهاد الاما م امير المؤمنين عليه السلام ثم جمعت فتكّون منها هذا الكتاب. والمؤلّف رحمه الله قد أنصف نفسه وأنصف عمله حينما اعترف — في المقدّمة - بانّ كتابه هذا لا يمثّل الاّ القليل في مثل هذا الموضوع الخطير، الواسع الجانب والمتشّعب المناحي، لاسيّما وانّ المؤلّف لم يقدّر له أن يبذل من الجهد الاقدر ما يبذل لا عداد محاضرات اربع، والا قدرما تستوعبه محاضرات اربع، بما لها من اطار زمنيّ وكلاميّ محدّد لا يمكنه أن يتجاوزه، والا ماسمح للمؤلّف وقنه الحافل بمراجعة هذه المحاضرات واعدادها للنّشر.

- ٣ -

والحمد لله الذي وفق المؤلّف رحمه الله للمدى الدي بلغه فيما تناوله من بحوث ودر اسات ترجع الى قوّة الجذب وقوّة الدّفع في شخصيّة امير المؤمنين عليه السلام، شأنه في هذا شأنه فيما تناوله من بحوث وما قام به من دراسات، ونحن - ويتّفق معنا عامّة القرّاء - قد رأينا في الكتاب فكرا اسلاميا عاليا، وعرضا تاريخيّا بديعا، وطر افة وابداعا - ضمن الاطار المحدود الذي ضيغت فيه بحوث الكتاب - ولهذا عزمنا على القيام بترجمته الى الانجليّزية، وعهدنا في ذلك الى مترجم خبير نحمد الله على أنه وفّق ايضالأن اكسب التّرجمة من الطّرافة والبراعة ما جعلها في مستوى النصّ الفارسيّ الذي جادت به براعة العلامة المطهري ومقدرته وقابليّاته.
ونحمد الله على ان وفّقنا لنشر الكتاب في ترجمته الانجليّزية ومن الله نسأل واليه نبتهل أن يجعل عملنا خالصا لوجهه الكريم، و أن يوفقنا لخير ما يوفّق له الصالحين من عباده انّه. نعم المولى ونعم النصير.

١٥/٨/١٤٠١ — المؤسسة العالمية للخدمات الاسلامية
١٨/٦/١٩٨١ — (لجنة التأليف و الترجمة والنشر)
طهران— ايران

PREFACE

-1-

This book, whose original title is *Jādhibah wa dāfi'ah-e 'Alī 'alayhi 's-salām* [lit. "The Attraction and Repulsion of 'Alī (a.s.)", or "The Power of Attraction and the Power of Repulsion of 'Alī (a.s.)"] is one of the important works of the late, great scholar ash-Shaykh Murtaḍā Muṭahharī, the Iranian writer, may Allāh have mercy upon him. The writer has himself given his explanation of this title in his introduction and in various places in the book, so there is no need for us to explain it any further.

We should not, however, overlook the fact that someone's power of attraction for those who love and help him, and even those who give themselves for him, and, on the other hand; his power of repulsion which create for that person opponents, enemies and even people who wish to kill him (we use the terms attraction and repulsion just as the author has), are for the primary factors in that person, but are two terms which summarise the multiple factors and effects which manifest themselves in him.

One set of these factors is the "essential" or "inward" ones which are found in that person and which are responsible for bringing people to love and help him, or to oppose and hate him. At the same time, there are essential factors which exist in the helpers or enemies themselves, which act together with the first set of factors to produce that love or eninity. There arc also external factors which strengthen the effects of these "essential" ones, or constitute obstacles to their fulfilment.

Now, if we consider the personality under discussion free from the context of his times, but rather as a man of all ages and times, we shall necessarily find some factors in addition to those related to his own time, which will be connected with his historical existence in its fully human sense. Fither these additional factors will augment the original ones, or else they will weaken them. The most important of these historical factors is the list of those who have loved, and have given themselves, for him, and their personalities, and the list of his opponents and enemies, and their personalities. and these lists are continually being added to as time proceeds and as centuries and generations succeed one another.

This becomes even more important when we consider a personality of the stature of Amīr al-mu'minīn (a.s.), where we find in his pure person the noblest human characteristics combined with the greatest Divine gifts, and in his Shī'ahs and enemies the strongest faith in the Divine Message combined with faith in mankind and its supreme mission, on the one hand and, on the other, hostility to the Divine Message combined with disbelief in mankind and a rising up against them.

If we take note of the above points, we can gain a clear idea of the great amount of energy that needs to be expended. the extent of the research and the depth of study which must be undertaken before it is possible for someone to do justice to the subject, so that a worthy result may he obtained from all the various aspects of his preliminary investigations.

-2-

This book, as the scholarly author, may Allāh have mercy on him, points out himself, developed out of four lectures originally given in connections with the commemoration of the martyrdom of al-Imām Amīr al-mu'minīn (a.s.). They were collected together and published in the form of this book. The author, may Allāh have mercy on him, was only doing justice to himself and to his work when he admitted, in his introduction, that his book is only a sample from his immense subject whose dimensions are broad and multi-faceted. It is our misfortune that the author found himself unable to expound any further on this great subject than these four lectures, which were circumscribed within the framework of the particular limited temporal and circumstantial events in which he found himself, except to the extent that the pressures of his responsibilities allowed him to review the material for publication.

-3-

Praise be to Allāh Who has caused the author, may Allāh have mercy on him, to succeed to the extent that he did in proceeding with his discussion, which relates to the powers of attraction and repulsion of Amīr al-mu'minīn (a.s.). He was fortunately able in this work to reach the same high level which he sustained in his other works. When we saw the great Islamic thinking, the clear historical presentation, the originality and novel exposition which are present in this book and about which the generality of readers are in agreement with us, and which exist despite the limitations inposed upon him, we decided to have the book translated into English. We gave it to an expert translator, whom, we thank Allāh, was able to translate it into hnglish with similar originality and skill to that which the scholar Muṭahharī manifested in the original text.

We praise Allāh that we have succeeded in publishing this book in an English version. We ask Allāh, and supplicate Him, that He may cause our work to be only in pure devotion to Him, and that He may cause us to succeed in the best thing in which He causes His virtuous slaves to succeed. For He is the best Guide and the best Artisan.

WORLD ORGANIZATION FOR ISLAMIC SERVICES,
(*Board of Writing, Translation and Publication*).

15/8/1401
18/6/1981
Tehran — Iran.

FOREWORD

The great, expansive personality of Amīr al-mu'minīn (Commander of the Believers), 'Alī - may peace be upon him - is broader and more multi-faceted than anything that one person can enter into in all its aspects and parts, or bring his restless mind to reflect. For a single individual, the most that is possible is that he choose one or several specific, limited areas for study and research, and content himself with that.

One of the aspects and areas of the being of this great individual is the effect he had on people, either positive or negative, or, in other words, his powerful "attraction and repulsion", which still now exerts its active influence, and it is with this that we shall be concerned in this book.

The personalities of individuals are not all the same in the reaction they produce in spirits and souls. The weaker the personality, the fewer minds it engages and the fewer hearts it excites and agitates. The greater and more powerful it is, the more it excites and provokes a reaction in the mind, although the reaction may be positive or negative.

Those personalities who excite minds and provoke a reaction are spoken of everywhere, they are the subjects of debates and disputes, they become the themes of poetry, painting and other arts, and the heroes of stories and other writings. These are all things which are true to the greatest extent in the case of 'Alī (a.s.)[1] and in this respect he has no rival, or at least very few rivals. It is said that Muḥammad ibn Shahrāshub al-Māzandarānī, who was one of the greatest Shī'ite scholars of the 7th century A.H. (13th century A.D.), had a thousand books with the title "*Manāqib*" (Noble Virtues), in his library, all written about 'Alī

1. (a.s.): is the abbreviation of the Arabic phrase *'alay-hi/ha/ himu 's-salām* (may peace be upon him/her/them).

(a.s.), at the time he wrote his own famous "*Manāqib*".[2] This is one indication of how much the exalted personality of the master has engaged minds throughout history.

The basic mark of distinction of 'Alī (a.s.) and other people who are bright with the rays of Truth is that as well as engaging people's minds and occupying their thoughts, they give light, warmth, love, joy, faith and strength to their Hearts.

Philosophers like Socrates, Plato, Aristotle, Ibn Sīnā or Descartes are also heroes of the mastering of ideas and the exercise of the mind. The leaders of social revolutions, especially in the last two centuries, have, to a greater extent, created a kind of adoration among their followers. The shaykhs of Sufism from time to time bring their followers so far into the stage of "submission" that if "the keeper of the tavern" gives the cue, they will stain their prayer-rugs with wine.[3] But in none of these cases do we see fervour and ardour combined with gentleness, kindness, sincerity and compassion as history has shown among the followers of 'Alī. If the Safavids made dervishes into a war-like army of skilled fighters, they did so in the name of 'Alī, not in their own.

Spritual goodness and beauty, which love and sincerity bring about, is one thing; supremacy, benefit, and what is of advantage in life, which is what the social leader deals in, or intellect and philosophy, which is what the philosopher deals in, or the establishing of "sovereignty" and "power" which is what the gnostic deals in, is something else.

There is a well-known story that one of Ibn Sīnā's students said to his

2. 3 vols., Najaf, 1376/ 1956.

3. See Ḥāfiẓ:

Let wine upon the prayer-mat flow.
An if the taverner bids so;
Whose wont is on this road to go
Its ways and manners well doth know.
(transl. A. J. Arberry, in *Fifty Poems of Ḥāfiẓ*, Cambridge, 1947, p. 83)

teacher that if, with his extraordinary understanding and intellegence, he were to make a claim to prophecy, people would gather round him. but Ibn Sīnā said nothing, till once, when they were on a journey together in wintertime, Ibn Sīnā awoke from his sleep one morning at dawn, woke up his student, and told him he was thirsty and to go and fetch some water. The student procrastinated and made excuses: however much Ibn Sīnā persisted, the student was not prepared to leave his warm bed in the cold winter. At that moment the cry of the muazzin called out from the minaret: *Allāhu akbār, Allāhu akbār*. . . . Ibn Sīnā saw that this was a good opportunity to give the answer to his student, so he said: "You, who averred that if I made claim to be a prophet people would believe in me, look now and see how the command I just gave to you, who have been my student for years and have benefited from my lessons, has not even had enough effect to make you leave your warm bed to fetch me some water. But this muezzin has obeyed the four hundred year old command of the Prophet, got up from his warm bed, climbed up to this height and borne witness to the unity of God and to his Prophet. Look and see how great the difference is!"

Philosophers produce students, not followers; social leaders create followers but not complete men; *quṭbs* and shaykhs of Sufism make "lords of submission", not active fighters for Islam.

In 'Alī we find the characteristics of the philosopher, the characteristics of a revolutionary leader, the characteristics of a Sufi shaykh and some of the characteristics of prophets. His school is the school of the intellect and thought, the school of revolution, the school of submission and discipline, and the school of goodness, beauty, ecstacy and movement.

Before he became the just leader (*imām*) of others, and behaved with justice towards them, 'Alī (a.s.) was himself a harmonised, equilibrated being; he had gathered together the perfections of humanity. He possessed both a deep and far reaching mind, and tender and overflowing affections; he had both perfection of body and perfection of spirit; in the night, in worship, he cut himself off from everything else, and during the day he was active among the people. In the daytime, people saw his kindness and altruism, and listened to his advice, counsel and wise words at night, the stars looked down on the tears of his worship and the heavens heard his prayers of love. He was both a learned man and a wise man, both a gnostic and a leader of society, both a man who denied his self and a soldier, both a judge and a worker, both a speaker and a writer. In sum, in all senses of the word he was a perfect man with all his attractiveness.

* * * * *

The present book is a collection of four lectures which were delivered between the 18th and 21st of the blessed month of Ramaḍān 1388 A.H. (1969 A.D.) in the Ḥusaynīyah-e Irshād, in Tehran. The book consists of an intoduction and two parts. In the introduction the generalities of attraction and repulsion in their broader sense, and the "attraction" and "repulsion" of men in particular, have been discussed. In the first part, the power of attraction of 'Alī (a.s.), which has, and always will, pull the hearts of people towards him, its philosophy, advantages and results, is the subject of discussion, and, in the second part, his powerful repelling effect, and how he strongly warded off and drove away certain elements, is examined and explained. It is shown that 'Alī (a.s.) was a man with these twin powers, and that everyone who wants to be taught in his way must possess these twin powers.

It is not enough just to point to the dual powers of this path in order to make it known. In this book we have tried to show, as far as possible, what kind of individuals were attracted by his force of attraction, and what type of person was warded off by his force of repulsion. How often have we, who claim to follow the way of 'Alī, pushed away the very people that 'Alī attracted, and attracted those who were repulsed by him. In the part on 'Alī's force of repulsion, we have contented ourselves with a discusssion of the Khawārij, but since there are other groups which were subject to this force of his, perhaps another time, or at least in a future printing of this book, this deficiency, as well as the other deficiencies of the book, will be amended.

The trouble of correcting and completing the lectures has been borne by the erudite Mr. Fatḥullāh Umidī. Half the book owes its existence to his stylish pen, for, after extracting it from recorded tapes, he wrote it again, occasioinally correcting and improving it. The other half of it is the writing of this scholar himself, or, sometimes, after his appropriate corrections, the addition of some points by myself. I trust that on the whole it will be useful and instructive. We beseach Allāh, the Exalted to make us true followers of 'Alī (a.s.).

Murtaḍā Muṭahharī.

11th Isfand, 1349 Sh.
4th Muḥarram, 1391 A.H.
2nd March, 1971 A. D.
Tehran – IRAN.

بسم الله الرحمن الرحيم

وَالْمُؤْمِنُونَ وَالْمُؤْمِنَاتُ بَعْضُهُمْ أَوْلِيَاءُ بَعْضٍ ۚ يَأْمُرُونَ بِالْمَعْرُوفِ وَيَنْهَوْنَ
عَنِ الْمُنكَرِ وَيُقِيمُونَ الصَّلَاةَ وَيُؤْتُونَ الزَّكَاةَ وَيُطِيعُونَ اللَّهَ وَرَسُولَهُ ۚ أُولَٰئِكَ
سَيَرْحَمُهُمُ اللَّهُ ۗ إِنَّ اللَّهَ عَزِيزٌ حَكِيمٌ ﴿التوبة، ٧١﴾

And the believers, the men and the women, are friends to one another: they bid to what is good, and forbid what is wrong; they perform the prayer, and pay zakat, and they obey Allāh and His Messenger. Those - upon them Allāh will have mercy; Allāh is All-mighty, Allwise. (9:71)

الْمُنَافِقُونَ وَالْمُنَافِقَاتُ بَعْضُهُم مِّن بَعْضٍ ۚ يَأْمُرُونَ بِالْمُنكَرِ وَيَنْهَوْنَ عَنِ
الْمَعْرُوفِ ﴿التوبة، ٦٧﴾

The hypocrites, the men and the women, are as one another; they bid to what is wrong, and forbid what is good. (9:67)

INTRODUCTION

The Law of Attraction and Repulsion
Attraction and Repulsion in the World of Man
Differences Between People as Regards Attraction and Repulsion
ʿAlī : One Man With the Two Powers

THE LAW OF ATTRACTION AND REPULSION

The law of "attraction and repulsion" is a law which holds sway throughout the entire order of creation. From the point of view of the scientific school of today, man is quite sure that not a single atom of the world of existence is outside the governance of general attraction, and none can escape it. From the largest of the world's bodies and masses to the smallest of its atoms, all possess this enigmatic force called the force of attraction, and all are, in some way, influenced by it.

Ancient man did not discover the universal general law of attraction, but he did discover attraction in some bodies, and recognised some things as symbolic of this force, such as the magnet and amber. Even so, he did not know of the relationship of attraction between these things and all other things, as he was only acquainted with a particular relationship: that of the magnet to iron, or amber to straw.

Each one of the atoms on atoms which exist between
this earth and the heaven
Is, for its own kind, like straw and amber.[1]

Apart from this, there was no talk of the force of attraction with other inanimate bodies: only about the earth was it asked why it was fixed in the middle of the havens. It was believed that the earth was suspended in the middle of space and was attracted on every side, and that since this pull was from all sides, it naturally stayed in the middle and did not incline to any one side. Some people believed that the heavens did not attract the earth, but rather that they repelled it, and that, since the force influencing the earth was equal on all sides, the result was that the earth was fixed in a particular spot and never changed its place.

There was also general belief in the faculty for attraction and repulsion in the case of plants and animals, in the sense that it was recognised that

1. Rūmī, *Mathnavī*, bk. 6.

these had three basic faculties: the nutritive faculty, the faculty of growth, and the faculty of reproduction. For the nutritive faculty, they believed there were some subsidiary faculties: attractive, repulsive, digestive and retentive. It was said that there was in the stomach a force of attraction which pulled food towards itself, or, occasionally, when it did not accept the food, excreted or repelled it;[2] and similarly it was said that there was a power of attraction in the liver which drew water towards itself.

The stomach draws in bread to its resting place,
The heat of the liver draws in water.[3]

ATTRACTION AND REPULSION IN THE WORLD OF MAN

The meaning of attraction and repulsion here is not the attractions and repulsions to do with sex, although these too are a particular kind of attraction and repulsion, for they have nothing to do with our discussion and form an independent object of enquiry. Rather the meaning here is the attractions and repulsions which exist among individual human beings in the arena of social life. In human society there are also some forms of cooperation which are based on the sharing of benefits, but these too, of course, are not, within the scope of our discussion.

The greatest proportion of friendships and affections, or enmities and hatred are all manifestations of human attraction and repulsion. These attractions and repulsions are based on general resemblance and similarity, or opposition and mutual aversion.[4] In fact, the basic cause of attraction and repulsion must be looked for in general resemblance and contrariety (*taḍādd*), just as in the discussions of metaphysics it has been proved that general resemblance is the cause of union.

2. Nowadays, however, the structure of the body is thought to be more like a machine, and the action of excretion is likened to a pump.
3. Rūmī, *Mathnavī, ibid.*
4. As opposed to what is said concerning electric currents, where two similar poles repel each other, while two unlike ones attract each other.

Sometimes two human beings attract each other, and their hearts wish for them to be friends and companions one with the other. There is a secret in this, and the secret is nothing other than general resemblance. Unless there is a similarity between these two persons, they cannot attract one another and move towards friendship with each other. In general the nearness of both of them is evidence for a kind of similarity and general resemblance between them.

In the second book of Rūmī's *Mathnavī* there is a fine story which illustrates this. A wise man saw a raven who had formed an affection for a stork. They perched together and flew together! Two birds of two different species: the raven had no similarity either in shape or in colour with the stork. The wise man was amazed that they were together. He went close and examined them and discovered that both of them had only one leg.

That wise Man said: "I saw companionship
Between a raven and a stock.
Amazed I was, and examined their condition
To see what sign of commonality I could find.
So up I crept, and, lo and behold!
I saw that both of them were lame."

This one-leggedness brought fellowship to two species of animal which were alien to each other. Human beings, too, will never become friends and companions with each other without some reason, just as they will never be enemies without a cause.

According to some, the root of these attractions and repulsions is need, and the elimination of need. They say that man is a creature who is in need, and that he is created essentially in want. He endeavours by his own relentless activity to till his emptiness and to supply his necessities, but this is impossible unless he joins with an ally and severs his linking relationship with society, so that he can take advantage from his ally by this means and protect himself from damage from some other group. And we will not find any inclination or aversion in man unless it springs from his instinct for taking advantage. According to this theory, the experiences of life and the structure of his primordial nature have brought man up to be attracted and repelled, so that he is enthusiastic about what he reckons is good in life, and keeps away from himself what does not conform with his aims, but is unresponsive when faced by what is neither of these, is that which neither holds out any benefit for him nor is detrimental. In fact, attraction and repulsion are two fundamental pillars of the life of man, and to whatever degree these are reduced, disorder takes the place of order in his life. In the end the one who has the power to fill up the vacuums attracts others to himself, and the one who not only does not fill up these vacuums but rather adds to the vacuums drives people away from himself, and likewise with those who do neither.

DIFFERENCES BETWEEN PEOPLE AS REGARDS ATTRACTION AND REPULSION

In terms of attraction and repulsion in relation to other individuals, not all people are the same: indeed they can be divided up into various classes:

1. **Individuals who do not attract and do not repel:** No one likes them, nor is anyone their enemy; they incite no one's love, affection or attachment, nor anyone's hostility, envy, hatred or odium; they go among men indifferently, just as if a slab of rock were to be among them.

Such a creature is as nothing, produces no effect, a person in whom no positive thing exists either in terms of goodness or in terms of evil (the meaning of "positive" has to do not only with virtue - it has to do with wickedness too). He is an animal, he eats, he sleeps and walks among men. He is like a sheep which is no one's friend and no one's enemy, and if he is looked after, if he is given his water and grass, it is because his meat will be consumed after a while. He neither starts any wave of approval, nor any wave of disapproval. Such people form a group of worthless creatures, hollow and vacuous human beings, for man needs to love and to be loved, and we can also say that he needs to hate and to be hated.

2. **People who attract but do not repel:** They get on well with everybody, they establish cordial relations with all people, they make people of all classes their admirers. In life, everyone likes them, and no one disowns them, and when they die, the Muslims wash them with water from the spring of *Zamzam* in Mecca and bury them, while the Hindus cremate them.

   So accustom yourself to good and bad,
   So that after your death
   Muslims will wash you in the water of Zamzam,
   And the Hindus cremate you.[5]

According to the advice of this poet, in a society where half are Muslims and respect the corpse of a dead man, giving it *ghusl* (ablution for the dead), and maybe giving it *ghusl* in sacred water from *Zamzam* as a result of greater respect, and half are Hindus who cremate the dead and caste their ashes to the wind, one should live in such a way that Muslims accept you as one of theirs and want to wash you after death in water from *Zamzam*, and Hindus also accept you as one of theirs and want to cremate you after death.

It is often imagined that excellence of character, civility in social intercourse, or, in the language of today "being sociable," consists of just this, making all men one's friends.

5. 'Urfī was an Iranian poet (963/1555 - 999/1590) who travelled to India and frequented the Court of the Emperor Akbar.

However, this is not feasible for the man who has an aim, who follows a path, who, among men, persues a particular way of thinking or ideal, and does not consider his own advantage; such a man, like it or not, has only one face, he is decisive and explicit in his behaviour, unless, of course, he is a hypocrite and double-faced. For not all men think in the same way, or feel in the same way, and not everyone's preferences are of one kind; among men there are those who are just and those who are unjust, there is good and there is bad. Society has its equitable members, and its despotic members; there are just people, there are iniquitous people. These people cannot all love one person, one human being, who seriously persues one goal and thus collides with some of their interests. The only person who will succeed in attracting the friendship of all the various classes and the various idealisms is one who dissimulates and lies, and says and shows to each person what conforms to that person's liking. But if the person is sincere and follows a path, one group will automatically be his friend and another will similarly be his enemy. Any group which follows the same way as him will be pulled towards him, and any group which follows some different way will exclude him and will quarrel with him.

Some Christians. who present themselves and their religion as messengers of peace, believe that the perfect man possesses nothing but love, thus he has nothing but the power of attraction, and perhaps some Hindus also believe the same thing.

One of the things that is very striking in Hindu and Christian philosophy is love. They say that one must cultivate affection for all things and make one's love manifest, and when we come to love everyone what can possible prevent everyone from loving us - the bad will also love us, since they will have seen our love.

But these gentlemen should understand that it is not enough merely to be a man of love, one must also be a man with a path, just as Gandhi said: "This is my religion." Love must coincide with reality and, if it coincides with reality it will have some path which it follows, and following a way creates enemies, whether we wish it or not. In fact, it is the power of repulsion which incites one group to struggle and excludes another group.

Islam is also the law of love. The Qur'ān presents the Holy Prophet as a mercy for all Being: (*raḥmatan li'l-'ālamin*)

وَمَا أَرْسَلْنَاكَ إِلَّا رَحْمَةً لِّلْعَالَمِينَ

We have not sent thee, save as a mercy unto all beings

(Anbiyā', 21:107).

This means that you (i.e., the Prophet) should be a mercy even for the most dangerous enemy, and should love even them.[6]

However the love which the Qur'ān commands does not mean that we should act towards everyone in conformity with what he likes and what is pleasing to him, that we should behave towards him in such a way that makes him happy and necessarily attracted towards us. Love does not mean that we leave everyone free to follow their inclinations, or still more that we should approve of their inclinations; this is not love, rather it is hypocrisy and double-dealing. Love is that which coincides with reality, it causes one to reach good, and sometimes those things which bring us to the good take a form that does not attract the love and affection of the other person. How many individuals there are to whom

6. It shows, what is more, that he loved all things, even animals and innanimate things. Thus we can see in the history of his life that all the things he used had special names. His horses, his swords and his turbans all had special names, and the only reason for this was that all existent things were the objects of the expression of his love and affection; it is as if he considered everything to have an individuality. History bears no trace of any human being with this manner apart from him, and this manner in fact shows that he was the paradigm of human love. When he passed by the mountain of Uḥud, he looked at it with kindness through his radiant eyes and with a look overflowing with love, and said: *jabal yuhibbunā wa nahibbuh* - "It is a mountain which loves us and we love it." He was a man in whose love mountains and stones also shared.

someone is loving in this way and who, when they observe that this love is at odds with their own inclinations, become hostile instead of appreciative. Besides, rational and intelligent love is that in which is the good and interest of the whole of mankind, not the good of one individual or one special group. There are many things which can be done to bring good to individuals and to show love for them which are the very same things which bring evil to society as a whole and may be its enemy.

We can find many great reformers in history who endeavoured to ameliorate the situation of society and smooth its sufferings, but who, in exchange, received no acknowledgement but animosity and persecution from people. So it is not the case that everywhere love attracts; indeed love sometimes manifests itself as a great repulsion which brings together whole societies against a man.

'Abdu 'r- Raḥmān ibn Muljam was one of the most adamant enemies of 'Alī, and 'Alī understood well that this man was a very dangerous opponent. Sometimes, even, others would say to him that he was a dangerous man, and that he should get rid of him. But 'Alī asked in reply, "Should I punish before the crime? If he is my murderer, I cannot kill my own murderer: he is to murder me, not I him." It was about this person that 'Alī said:

أُرِيْدُ حَيَاتَهُ وَيُرِيْدُ قَتْلِي

> *I want him to live; he wants to kill me.*[7] (i.e., "I have love for him, but he is my enemy and has malevolent designs against me.")

Secondly, love is not the only healing drug for mankind; roughness is also necessary for certain tastes and temperaments, and conflict, repelling and driving away are also necessary. Islam is both the religion of attraction and love and the religion of repelling and retribution (*niqmah*).[8]

---

7. *Biḥāru 'l-anwār*, vol. 42, pp. 193-194 (Tehran, new edition).

8. Perhaps we should say that retributions are also a manifestation of ⇒

3. **People who repel but do not attract:** they make enemies but they make no friends. These are also deficient people, and it shows that they are deficient in positive human qualities, for if they partook of human qualities they would have groups, even if they were small in number, who were their supporters and who were attached to them. For there are always good people among humanity, however small their number may be. Even if all men were worthless and unjust, their hostility would be a proof of truth and justice, but it is never the case that all men are bad, just as they are never all good. Naturally, the bad in someone who has an enemy in everyone is to

⇐ affectionate sentiments and love. In *du'ās* (supplication to God) we read: *yā man sabaqat raḥmatuh ghaḍabah* - "Oh You in whom mercy and love have taken precedence over anger", i.e., because You want to be merciful You are angry; otherwise, if that mercy and love did not exist, neither would the anger.

It is like a father who becomes angry with his son because he loves him and is concerned for his future. If his son opposes him, he becomes angry, and he may sometimes beat him, but despite however much ruder behaviour he may see from others' sons and children, he never gets worked up by it. In the case of his own son he becomes angry, because he has affection for him; but in the case of others. he does not become angry, for he has no affection.

On the other hand, affections sometimes deceive; that is to say, there are sentiments which the intellect cannot truly understand, as the Qur'ān says:

وَلَا تَأْخُذْكُم بِهِمَا رَأْفَةٌ فِي دِينِ اللَّهِ

In the matter of God's religion (i.e., the divine laws) let no tenderness for them (the offenders) seize you (an-Nur, 24: 2).

The reason for this is that Islam, while it demonstrates concern and affection for individuals, is also concerned about society. The greatest sin is a sin which appears small in the eyes of man and seems to be of no importance. Amīr al-mu'minīn said:

أَشَدُّ الذُّنُوبِ مَا اسْتَهَانَ بِهِ صَاحِبُهُ

The most serious sin is the sin which the sinner imagines to be slight and insignificant. (*Nahju 'l-balāghah*, Saying no. 340).

The spread of sin is something which hides the seriousness of the sin from people's sights, and makes it seem nothing in the eyes of the individual.

be found within himself, for otherwise how could it be possible for there to be good in the human spirit and then for this man to have no friends. There are no positive sides to the personalities of such individuals: even in their villainous aspects their persons are sour throughout, and they are sour for everyone. There is nothing in them which is sweet even if it be only to a few.

'Alī (a.s.) said:

أَعْجَزُ النَّاسِ مَنْ عَجَزَ عَنِ اكْتِسَابِ الْإِخْوَانِ، وَ أَعْجَزُ مِنْهُ مَنْ ضَيَّعَ مَنْ ظَفِرَ بِهِ مِنْهُمْ

The most powerless person is he who is unable to find any friends, and more powerless than these is the one who loses his friends and remains alone.[9]

4. **People who both attract and repel:** they are people travelling a path, who act in the way of their beliefs and principles; they draw groups of people towards themselves, they take a place in people's hearts as someone loved and wanted. But they also repel certain groups from themselves and drive them away. They make friends as well as eneinies; they encourage agreement as well as disagreement.

Such people are also of several kinds, for sometimes both their power of attraction and their power of repelling are strong, sometimes they are both weak, and sometimes there is a difference between them. There are some people with such a personality that their powers of attracting and repelling are both strong, and this is related to flow strong the positive and negative degrees in their spirits are. Of course, strength also has degrees, up to the point where the friends that have been attracted will ransom their souls and give themselves up entirely for the cause; and the enemies will also become so head-strong that they will give their lives in their own cause. And it may become so intense that centuries

9. *Nahju 'l-balāghah*, Saying no. 11.

after the death of that person their attraction and repelling will still be effective in people's minds and will exercise a wide influence. This three-dimensional attraction and repelling are among the particular characteristics of the *awliyā'*, (the "friends" of Allāh), just as the three-dimensional invitations to the way of Allāh are peculiar to the chain of the prophets.

In this respect, it must be seen what kinds of people are attracted and what kinds repelled. For example, sometimes those with knowledge are attracted, and those who are ignorant are repelled, and sometimes *vice versa.* Sometimes noble and civilised people are attracted and the evil and the wicked are repelled, and sometimes *vice versa.* Thus, friends and enemies, the attracted and the repelled, each one is a clear proof of the essence of such a person.

It is not sufficient merely to have the powers of attracting and repelling, or even that they sould be strong, in order that a person's character should become lauded, rather the cause of this is the character itself, and no one's character is a proof of goodness. All the world's leaders, even criminals such as Changīz Khān, Ḥajjāj and Mu'āwiyah, were people who had both the power to attract and the power to repel. Not unless there are positive points in someone's spirit he can never make thousands of soldiers obedient to him, and subdue their wills; not unless someone has the power of leadership can he gather people around himself to such a degree.

The Iranian king Nādir Shāh (b. 1100/1688, reigned 1148/1736. d. 1160/1747) was such a person. He cut off so many heads and had so many eyes gouged out of their sockets, but his personality was extraordinarily strong. From a defeated and plundered Iran at the end of the Safavīd period he created an army at great cost, and, just like a magnet that attracts iron-fillings, fighting men collected round him who not only saved Iran from foreign powers, but went to the furthermost parts of India and brought new territories under the rule of Iran.

Thus every person attracts his own kind, and drives away those unlike him. A just and noble person attracts towards himself benevolent people who strive for righteousness, and drives away from himself sensual, money-loving, hypocritical people. A criminal person attracts criminals around himself, and repels those who are good.

And, as we pointed out, there is another difference in the strength of the power of attraction. Just as is said about Newton's gravity, that the degree of pull and attraction becomes greater in proportion to the size of the mass of the body and in inverse proportion to the size of the intervening distance, so also among men there is variation in the power of attraction and pull which derives from the individual who has that attraction.

'ALĪ ONE MAN WITH TWO POWERS

'Alī is one of those persons who have both the power to attract and the power to repel, and his attraction and repelling are extremely strong. Perhaps no attraction and repelling as strong as 'Alī's can be found anywhere in any century or epoch. fie has had remarkable friends, truly historical persons, ready to sacrifice themselves, forbearing, burning with love for him like flames from a bonfire, and full of light. They deemed giving up their lives in his way to be their aim and their glory, and they became oblivious of everything in their friendship for him. Years, even centuries, have passed since the death of 'Alī, but this attraction still sends out the same rays of light, and people are still dazzled when they turn to it.

Throughout his life, noble and civilised individuals, worshippers of God, self-sacrificing, altruistic people, forbearing, merciful and just men, ready to serve the people, rotated round the axis of his existence so that the story of any one of them is instructive; and, after his death, during the times of the caliphate of Mu'āwiyah and the Umayyids, great masses of people were arrested for the crime of friendship to him and underwent the most severe tortures, but they did not give way in their friendship and love of ʿAlī and stood firm to the end of their lives.

With other individuals, everything dies when they die and become covered up, their corpses under the earth; but although men of truth die themselves, the following and love that they excite become more briliant with the passing of the centuries.

We read in history that years and centuries after the death of ʿAlī people courageously welcomed the arrows of his enemies.

Among all those who were attracted to, and captivated by, ʿAlī. we can notice Maytham at-Tammār who, twenty years after ʿAlī's martyrdom, spoke front his crucifixion of ʿAlī and his virtues and human qualities. In those days, when the entire Islamic people were being suffocated, when all freedoms were quashed and souls became prisoners in their own breasts, when a mortal silence showed like the mist of death of everyone's faces, this man shouted out from the crucifix for people to come and listen to what he would tell them about ʿAlī. People thronged round from all sides to hear what Maytham had to say. The powerful government of the Umayyids, which saw its own interests in danger, gave the order to put a gag in his mouth, and, after some days, put all end to his life. History bears many traces of this kind of devotion to ʿAlī.

These kinds of powerful attraction are not specific to any particular time; in all ages we see manifestations of them and their strong effectiveness.

There was a man called Ibn as-Sikkīt who was one of the great scholars and figures in Arabic literature, and his name is quoted among the authorities in the Arabic language like as-Sībawayh and others. He lived in the time of the ʿAbbāsid Caliph al-Mutawakkil, about two hundred years after ʿAlī's martyrdom. In the administration of al-Mutawakkil he was accused of being Shīʿah, but even then, because he was very learned and distinguished, al-Mutawakkil chose him as a teacher for his own children. One day, when al-Mutawakkil's children came to him, and Ibn as-Sikkīt was present and had that day apparently given them an examination in which they had acquitted themselves well, al-Mutawakkil showed his pleasure with Ibn as-Sikkīt, but perhaps because of misgivings due to having heard that he had learnings towards Shī'ite Islam, asked Ibn as-Sikkīt whether the two in front of him (i.e. his two sons) were dearer to him or Ḥasan and Ḥusayn, the two sons of 'Alī.

Ibn Sikkīt was greatly disturbed by this question and comparison and became very agitated. he asked himself whether this proud man had reached such a degree that he had begun to compare his own two sons with Ḥasan and Ḥusayn. He told himself that it was his fault for having been so successful in their education. In reply to al-Mutawakkil he said:

> "By Allāh, I swear the 'Alī's slave, Qanbar is definitely dearer to me than these two and their father."

al-Mutawakkil gave the order to the assembled people that Ibn as-Sikkīt's tongue should be cut out from his throat.

History can tell of many completely overwhelmed people who involuntarily sacrificed their lives in the way of love for 'Alī. Where can such attraction be found? One cannot imagine that in all the world there is a parallel.

To the same degree, 'Alī had stubborn enemies, enemies who set people trembling at the sound of their names. 'Alī is not to be looked at as an individual, but rather as a whole philosophy. And it is for this reason that one group is attracted to him, and one is repelled. Indeed. 'Alī was a man of two powers.

* * * * *

Part One : The Power of Attraction in ʿAlī

POWERFUL ATTRACTIONS

In the introduction to the first volume of *The Seal of the Prophets* (*Khātim-e Payāmbarān*), it is written concerning the topic of calls to mankind:

> "The 'calls' that have occurred among humanity have not all been the same, and the rays of their effects have not been of (only) one kind.
>
> "Some calls and systems of thought are one-dimensional, and proceed in one direction: when they appear. they embrace a broad spectrum of people, millions of people become adherents, but then after their time comes to an end they close shop and are entrusted to oblivion.
>
> "Some are two-dimensional, their rays spread out in two directions. While they embrace a broad spectrum of people, and also progress for some time, their range is not confined to the spatial dimension and also extend into the temporal dimension.
>
> "And some others progress in a multitude of dimensions. Not only do we see them attract a broad range of people from human societies and influence them and notice the effect of their influence on every continent, but we also see that they embrace the temporal dimension, that is to say. they are not confined to one time or era. They rule in all their might century after century. Also, they take root in the depths of the human spirit, and the very core of people's hearts is under their authoritative control; they rule in the profundity of the soul and take the reins of the emotions into their hands. This kind of three-dimensional call is the exclusivity of the chain of the prophets.
>
> "What intellectual or philosophical schools of thought can be found which, like the world's great religions, exert their authority over hundreds of millions of people for thirty centuries, or twenty centuries, or, at the minimum, fourteen centuries, and sink deep into their innermost core."

Forces of attraction are also like this: sometimes one, sometimes two, and sometimes three-dimensional.

'Alī's power of attraction was of the last kind. Not only did it attract a broad range of human society, but it was also not limited to one or two centuries; rather, it has continued and extended throughout time. It is a fact that it lights up the pages of the centuries and ages it has reached the depth and profundity of hearts and souls, in such a way that, after hundreds of years, when he is remembered and his moral virtues are heard of, tears of longing are shed, and the memory of his misfortunes is awakened to the extent that even his enemies are affected and their tears flow. This is the most powerful of attractive forces.

From here it can be understood that the link between man and religion is not a material one, but rather of another kind, the like of which link connects no other thing to the spirit of mankind.

If 'Alī had had no divine colouring and had not been a man of God, he would have been forgotten. The history of man bears traces of many champions, champions of speech, champions of knowledge or philosophy, champions of power and authority and champions in the battle-field, but all are forgotten by people, or else completely unknown.

But not only did 'Alī not die with his being killed, he became more alive. He spoke well when he said:

هَلَكَ خُزَّانُ الْأَمْوَالِ وَهُمْ أَحْيَاءٌ، وَالْعُلَمَاءُ بَاقُونَ مَا بَقِيَ الدَّهْرُ، أَعْيَانُهُمْ مَفْقُودَةٌ،
وَأَمْثَالُهُمْ فِي الْقُلُوبِ مَوْجُودَةٌ

> *Those who amass wealth are dead even when they are alive, but those with knowledge will remain as long as the world remains. Their bodies may have disappeared, but their images continue to exist in the hearts.* (*Nahju 'l-balāghah*, Saying no. 47)

He said about his own character:

غَداً تَرَوْنَ أَيَّامِي، وَيُكْشَفُ لَكُمْ عَنْ سَرَائِرِي، وَتَعْرِفُونَنِي بَعْدَ خُلُوِّ مَكَانِي
وَقِيَامِ غَيْرِي مَقَامِي

Tomorrow, you will see these days of mine and unknown characteristics of mine will be revealed to you, and after my place has been vacated and someone else has occupied it you will know me. (*Nahju 'l-balāghah*, Sermon no. 149)

Iqbal wrote:

My, own age does not understand my deep meanings,
My Joseph is not for this market.
I despair of my old champions,
My Sinai burns for the sake of the Moses who is coming.
Their sea is silent, like dew,
But my dew is storm-ridden, like the ocean.
My song is of another world than theirs:
This bell calls other traverllers to take the road.
Many a poet was born after his death.
He opened our eyes when his own were closed,
And journeyed forth again front nothingness
Like roses blossoming over the earth of his grave.
No river will contain my Oman:
My flood requires whole seas to hold it.
Lightenings slumber within my soul.
I sweep over mountain and plain.
The fountain of Life hath been given me to drink,
I have been made an adapt of the mystery of Life.
No one hath told the secret which I will tell
Or threaded a pearl of thought like mine
Heaven taught me this lore,
I cannot hide it from my comrades.[1]

1. Muhammad Iqbāl: *The Secrets of the Self*, translation of R. A. Nicholson, 2nd revised ed., Lahore 1940.

In fact, 'Alī is like the laws of nature which remain unchanged by time. He is a well-sprint; of munificence which is never dry, but which rather increases day by day. In the words of Kahlil Gibran (Jubrān Khalīl Jubrān [1300/1883 - 1349/1931]), he was one of those personalities who was born before his time.

* * * * *

SHĪ'ISM, THE RELIGION OF LOVE

One of the greatest marks of distinction of Shī'ism over other sects is that its foundation and its bedrock is love. Right from the time of the Prophet who laid the basis of this sect there has been the whispering of love, when we hear from the words of the Prophet the sentence:

'Aliyyun wa shī'atuhu humu 'l-Fā'izun.
'Alī and his party (Shī'ah) will be the triumphant ones.[2]

we see that there was a group around 'Alī who were devoted to him, extremely fond of him and most affectionately drawn towards him. Thus Shī'ism is the religion of love and devotion: taking 'Alī as one's friend is the way of love. The element of love has completely penetrated Shī'ism, and the history of Shī'ism is joined in name with a chain of entirely unknown people, devoted, full of love and self-sacrificing.

Although 'Alī administered the Divine punishments to some, dealt with them with lashes and occasionally cut the hand of someone off in accordance with what is laid down by the Divine Law, they did not turn

2. In *ad-Durru 'l-manthūr*, under the seventh verse of Sūrah al-Bayyinah (90), Jalālu 'd-Dīn as-Suyūṭī narrates from Ibn 'Asākir that Jābir ibn 'Abdillāh al-Anṣārī said that he was in the presence of the Prophet when 'Alī also came in to him. The Prophet said: "I swear by He in Whose hand is my life that this man and his followers (Shiī'ah) will be saved on the Day of Resurrection." al-Manāwī relates this in two traditions in *Kunūzu 'l-ḥaqā'iq*, and al-Haythamī in *Majma'u 'z-zawā'id* and Ibn Ḥajar in *aṣ-Ṣawā'iqu 'l-muḥriqah* relates the same substantial meaning in different forms.

away from him and their love for him did not diminish in the slightest. He himself said:

> If I strike the nose of a believer with this sword of mine so that he will become my enemy, it will not create hostility and if I pour the (riches of the) whole world on the head of a hypocrite so that he may like me, he will never like me; because this has been decreed and laid down by the tongue of the Prophet when he said: "O 'Alī, the believer will never be your enemy and the hypocrite will never love you!"[3]

'Alī is the standard and criterion for assaying human nature and temperaments: he who has a sound nature and a pure temperament will never take offence at 'Alī, even though his sword may come down on his head, while he who has a diseased nature will never show any attachment to him, even if he does him great favours, for 'Alī is nothing but the embodiment of truth.

There was a friend of Amīr al-mu'minīn, a good and believing man, who unfortunately fell into error, and who had to be punished. Amīr al-mu'minīn cut off the fingers of his right hand. The man took hold of his cut hand, with the blood dripping from it, with his left hand, and went away. Ibn al-Kawwā', a seditious Khārijite, wanted to take advantage of this course of events for his own party and against 'Alī, so he came up to the man with an air of utter compassion and said: "Who cut your hand off?"

"The chief of the Prophet's successors," he said, "the leader of the untainted ones at the Resurrection, the most righteous among the believers, 'Alī ibn Abī Ṭālib, the Imām of right guidance, cutt off the fingers of my right hand . . . the first to reach the Gardens of Felicity, the hero of the brave, the avenger against the promoters of ignorance, the giver of zakat . . . the leader on the right and perfect path, the speaker of what is true and appropriate, the champion of Mecca, the steadfast exceller."

---

3. *Nahju 'l-balāghah,* Saying no. 42.

"Poor you!" said Ibn al-Kawwā', "He cut off your hand, and you extol him thus!"

"Why should I not extol him," he said, "now that his friendship is mixed with flesh and blood? I swear by God that he did not cut off my hand except with a right that God has established."[4]

This love and affection which we see in such a way in the history of 'Alī and his companions, makes us turn to the topic of love and its results.

* * * * *

THE ELEXIR OF LOVE

The Persian poets called love the "elexir" (*iksīr*). The alchemists believed that there existed a material in the world which they called the "elexir"[5] or "the philosopher's stone" (*kīmiya*) which could change one matter into another matter, and they searched after this for centuries. The poets took over the use of this terminology and said that the real "elexir" which has the power of transformation is love, because it is love which can transumute a substance. Love, absolutely, is the "elexir" and has the

4. *Biḥāru 'l-anwār*, vo1. 40, pp. 281-2 (new ed.); and Fakhru'd-Dīn ar-Rāzī, *at-Tafsīru '1-kabīr*, under verse 9, *Sūrah al-Kahf* ("Or dost thou think. . .").
5. In the Persian-Language dictionary *Burhān-e qāṭi'*, the following is written about "elexir" (*iksīr*): "It is a substance which melts down, combines and perfects; that is to say it makes gold from copper and useful drugs beneficial. It seems that "perfection" is also called "the elexir" metaphorically." It so happens that in love the same three properties are present - it "melts down", it "combines" and it "perfects" - but the well-known and famous metaphorical aspect of it is third one, its perfecting transformative power. Thus poets have sometimes called love by the name of "the doctor", "the drug (*dawā'*)", "Plato" or "Galen". In the prologue to the *Mathnavī* Rūmī writes:

Hail, O Love that bringest us good again -
Thou that art the physician of all our ills,
The remedy of our pride and vainglory,
Our Plato and our Galen!

(transl. Nicsholson, bk. 1, 1.23)

properties of the philosopher's stone, which changes one nature into another, and people also are different natures.

اَلنَّاسُ مَعَادِنٍ كَمَعَادِنِ الذَّهَبِ وَالفِضَّةِ

People are mines, like gold-mines and silver-mines.

It is love which makes the heart a heart, and if there is no love, there is no heart, just clay and water.

Every heart that is not aflame is no heart:
A frozen heart is nothing but a handful of clay.
O God! Give me a breast that sets ablaze,
And in that breast a heart, and that heart consumedwith fire.[6]

One of the effects of love is power; love is the power of glory, it makes the coward courageous.

A hen will keep its wings folded by its side as long as it is alone. It will strut about quite peaceably, looking about to find small worms to swallow. It will start at the slightest noise, and not stand its ground even in front of the weakest child. But when the same hen has chickens, love takes up its dwelling at the centre of its being and its character completely changes. The wings which were folded by its side are now lowered in a sign of preparation for defence, it assumes an aggressive posture, even the sound of its clucking becomes stronger and more courageous. Previously it fled at the possibility of danger, but now it attacks where there is that possibility, and it attacks bravely. This is love which displays the frightened hen in the form of a valiant animal.

Love makes the heavy and lazy nimble and cunning, and even makes the slow-witted astute. A boy and girl neither of whom, when they were single, found themselves thinking about anything except what was directly related to their own persons, see that they have become concerned about the fate of another being for the first time as soon as

6. From Vaḥshī Kirmānī, Iranian poet (- 991/1583).

they fall in love and set up a family environment. The radius of their wants extends; and when they become parents, their spirit completely changes. That heavy and lazy adolescent boy has now become active and mobile, and that girl who used not to get out of her bedclothes even during the day moves like lightning when site hears the cry of her child in the cradle. What is this power which has so galvanised the languor and weariness in these two young people? It is nothing but love.

It is love which turns the miser into a benefactor, and an impatient and intolerant person into someone with endurance and tolerance. It is love which gave the selfish bird which collected grain only with itself in mind and looked only after itself, the form of a generous creature which calls for its chickens when it finds a grain of corn; or which, by some wonderful power, makes the mother, who was until yesterday a spoiled child who just ate and slept and was irritable and impatient, persevering and forbearing when faced with hunger, lack of sleep and dishevelment, which gives her the patience to endure the hardships of motherhood.

The bringing into existence of tenderness in, and the removal of heaviness and coarseness from, the spirit, or, put in another way, the purification of the feelings, and also the unification and singleness of purpose and concentration, and the disappearance of distraction and dispersion are the strengths and, in the end, power which is produced by the coming together of all the resulting effects of love.

In the language of poetry and literature, when love is spoken of, we encounter one effect more than any other, and that is the power of love to bring inspiration, and its prodigality.

The nightingale learnt its song by the favour of the
rose, otherwise there would not have been
Any of this song and music fashioned from its beak.[7]

7. Ḥāfiẓ.

Although the favour of the rose is. if we attend only to the words, a matter outside the existence of the nightingale, it is in fact nothing but the force of love itself.

Do you imagine that Majnūn became deranged (majnūn) by himself?
It was the glance of Laylā that transported him among the stars.[8]

Love awakens sleeping powers, and frees chained and fettered forces. just like the splitting of the atom and the freeing of atomic power. It tires with inspiration and builds heroes - how many poets, philosophers and artists there have been who were created by a strong and powerful love.

Love perfects the soul and brings out astounding latent abilities. From the point of view of the powers of perception, it inspires, and from the point of view of the emotions, it strengthens the will and determination, and when it rises to its highest aspect it brings miracles and supernatural events into existence. It purifies the spirit from the tempers and humours of the body; or, in other words, love is a cathartic, it purges the base qualities arising from egotism, or from coldness and lack of warmth, such as envy, avarice, cowardice, laziness, conceited ness and self-admiration. It removes grudges and malevolence, although it is possible that deprivation of, and frustration in, love may produce, in their own turn, complexes and aversions.

By love, bitternesses became sweet,
By love, pieces of copper became gold.[9]

In the spirit, the effect of love is in terms of its development and thriving; in the body, in terms of melting and decomposition. The effect of love in the body is the complete opposite of what is in the spirit. In the body love is the cause of ruination, and the reason for pallor and emaciation in the body, for indisposition and disorder in the digestive and the nervous

8. 'Allāmah Ṭabā'ṭabā'ī.
9. Rūmī, *Mathnavī*.

systems. Perhaps all the effects which it has in the body are destructive; but in connection with the spirit it is not so - it depends on the object of love and how the person responds to that object. Leaving aside its social effects, it is predominantly perfecting in the spirit and the individual, because it produces strength, compassion, serenity, singleness of purpose, and determination; it abolishes weakness, meanness, annoyance, uncollectedness and dullness. It removes the confusions which are called *dassā* in the Qur'ān (91:10), meaning adulterations of purity with impurity, destroys deceit and purifies the cheat.

The spiritual way ruins the body,
And, after having ruined it, restores it to prosperity:
O happy the soul who, for love and ecstasy,
Gave up hearth and home, wealth and riches.
Ruined the house for the sake of the golden treasure,
And with that same treasure rebuilt it better;
Cut off the water and cleansed the river-bed.
Then caused drinking-water to flow in tire river-bed;
Cleft the skin and drew out the iron point-
Then fresh skin grew over it.
The perfect ones who are aware of the secret of reality
Are in ecstasy. bewildered. intoxicated and deranged with love.
Not bewildered in such wise that his back is towards Him,
But so bewildered that (they are) drowned and intoxicated with the Beloved.[10]

* * * * *

BREAKING DOWN THE BARRIERS

Love brings man out from egoism and self-love, irrespective of what kind of love it is - animal and sexual, animal and parental, or human - and irrespective of what qualities and excellences the loved-one has, whether

10. Adapted from Nicholson's translation of Rūmī, *Mathnavī*, bk. 1.

bold and valiant, artistic or wise, or whether her or she be in possession of a fine morality, social graces or other special attributes. Self-love is a limitation and a defensive barrier; love completely breaks down this defensive barrier to other than the self. Man is weak until he has gone outside his own self, he is timid, avaricious, covetous, misanthropic, quick-tempered, selfish and arrogant; his spirit gives out no spark or brilliancy, it has no vivacity or animation, it is always cold and cut off. However, as soon as he takes a step outside his "self" and breaks down his defensive barriers, these ugly habits and qualities are also destroyed.

Whoever's garment is torn by love
Is entirely cleansed ofcovetousness or blemish.[11]

Self-love, in the sense of something which must be eliminated, is not something which really exists. What we mean is that it is not a real, existing fondness for himself which man must do away with so that he can become liberated from "self-love". It makes no sense for a human being to try not to like himself; esteem for oneself which we can call "amour-propre" has not been mistakenly overlooked so that we have to throw that out. The reform and perfecting of man does not mean that, let us suppose, a series of extraneous matters in his existence are thought up and then that these extraneous and detrimental things must be eliminated. In other words the reform of man does not lie in reducing him, it lies in perfecting and adding to him. The responsibility that creation has assigned to man's charge is in the direction of the course of creation, that is, in perfection and growth, not in decrease and reduction. The struggle with self-love is the struggle with the limitations of the self. This self must be expanded; this defensive structure, which has been placed round the self and which sees every other thing, apart from what is connected to itself as a person or an individual, as foreign, "not me", and alien to itself, must be broken down. The personality must expand to take in every other human being, if not the whole of the universe of creation. Thus the struggle with self-love is the struggle with the

11. Rūmī, *Mathnavī*, bk. 1.

limitations of the self; and therefore self-love is nothing else but a limitation of the conceptual and motivational process. Love turns man's affections and drives towards what is outside his self, it enlarges his existence and changes the focal point of his being. For the same reason, love is a great moral and educative factor, on condition that it is well guided and is correctly used.

* * * * *

CONSTRUCTIVE OR DESTRUCTIVE?

When affection for an individual or a thing reaches the summit of intensity so that it conquers man's existence and becomes the absolute ruler over his being, it is called love. Love is the peak of affection and the sentiments.

But it should not be imagined that what is called by this name is of only one kind; it is of two completely opposite kinds. Those things which are called its good effects are connected with one of its kinds, but its other kind has completely destructive and opposite effects.

The sentiments of man are of various kinds and degrees; some of them are in the category of the passions, especially the sexual passions, and are of those, aspects which are shared by man and the other animals, with the difference that in man, for a particular reason the explanation of which cannot be appropriately undertaken now, it reaches its peak and takes on an indescribable intensity; and for this reason it is called love. It never takes on this form among animals, but, in any case, in its reality and essence, it is nothing but a torrent, a bursting forth, a tempest of the passions. It originates from the source of sexuality, and reaches its end there too. Its rise and fall are, too a large degree, connected to the physiological activity of the genital organs and naturally to the years of youth; it diminishes and eventually ceases altogether with an increase in age, on the one hand, and, on the other, with satiation and separation.

A youth who feels himself a-quiver at the sight of a beautiful face or a tress of hair, or who feels a frisson when touched by a tender hand, should know that there is nothing more operating here than a material, animal process. This kind of love comes quickly and goes quickly. It cannot be depended on, nor recommended, it has dangers and it kills virtue. It is only by the help of modesty and piety and not becoming abandoned to it that it may profit a human being; that is, in itself, it is a power which leads man towards no virtue. But it gives a strength and a perfection to the spirit, if it penetrates into a man's being, is met with the power of modesty and piety, and if the spirit tolerates the pressure of it - provided it does not succumb to it.

Humans have another variety of sentiments which, in their reality and essence, differ from the passions; it is better to call these noble sentiments, or in the language of the Qur'ān, "love and mercy" (*muwaddah wa raḥmah* [see 30:21]).

As long as man is under the control of his passions, he has not gone out from his self, he seeks a person or a thing whom he is attracted to for himself, and he wants it dearly. If he thinks about a love-object, it is with the idea of how he might profit from being united with it, or at the most how he can derive enjoyment from it. It is obvious that such a state cannot be the perfecter or the educator of man's spirit, or refine it.

However, man occasionally comes under the effect of his higher human sentiments; his loved-one receives respect and eminence in his eyes, he seeks that person's happiness. He is prepared to sacrifice himself for that person's desires. This kind of sentiment brings purity, sincerity, tenderness, compassion and altruism into existence, as opposed to the first kind which creates crudeness, savagery and criminality. The kindness and affection of a mother for her child is of this second kind. Devotion to, and love of, the pure ones and the men of God, as also patriotism and the love of principles, are also from the same category.

It is this kind of sentiment from which, if it reaches its summit and perfection, all the aforementioned good effects result; and it is this kind which gives dignity, distinction and greatness to the spirit, in contrast to the first kind which brings wretchedness. Similarly it is this kind of love which is durable, and which becomes stronger and warmer with union, as opposed to the first kind which is not permanent and whose graveyard union is reckoned to be.

In the Qur'ān, the relationship between a man and wife is described as "love and compassion"[12], and this is a very great point. It is an indication of the human and higher than-animal aspect of married life. It is an indication that the factors of the passions are not the only natural link in married life. The fundamental link is purity, sincerity and the union of two spirits; or, in other words, the thing which joins the married couple one to the other, and unites them, is compassion, mercy, purity and sincerity, not the passions, which also exist between animals.

In his own subtle way, Rūmī distinguishes between the passions and true love; he calls the former animal and the latter human. He says:

Wrath and passion are the attributes of beasts,
Love and compassion the attributes of man.
Thus Love is the characteristic of
Adam, missing in animals, a deficiency.

Materialist philosophers too have not been able to deny this spiritual state which, from several standpoints, has a non-material aspect, and which would not be in conformity with man and what is beyond him being material.

In *Marriage and Morals*, Bertrand Russell writes:

Work of which the motive is solely pecuniary cannot have this

12. وَمِنْ آيَاتِهِ أَنْ خَلَقَ لَكُم مِّنْ أَنفُسِكُمْ أَزْوَاجًا لِّتَسْكُنُوا إِلَيْهَا وَجَعَلَ بَيْنَكُم مَّوَدَّةً وَرَحْمَةً
And of His signs is that He created for you, of yourselves, spouses, that you might repose in them, and He has set between you love and compassion. (ar-Rūm, 30:21)

> value, but only work which embodies some kind of devotion, whether to persons, to things, or merely to a vision. And love itself is worthless when it is merely possessive; it is then on a level with work which is purely pecuniary. In order to have the kind of value which we are speaking, love must feel the ego of the beloved person as important as one's own ego, and must realise the other's feelings and wishes as though they were one's own.[13]

Another point which should be mentioned and carefully attended to is that we said that even loves of the passions may possibly become beneficial, and that occurs when they become linked to piety and modesty. That is to say, in connection with, on the one hand, separation and inaccessibility, and, on the other hand, purity and modesty, the pains and anguishes, pressures and difficulties to which the spirit is subjected bear good and beneficial results.

It is in this connection that the mystics say that allegorical love is turned in real love, i.e., love of the Essence of the One; and it is also in connection with this that the following tradition is narrated:

> *He who becomes a lover, who conceals (his love), who is chaste (in his love) and dies (in that state) has died as a martyr.*

However the point must not be forgotten that this kind of love, with all the advantages that may, under particular conditions, possibly be brought about, is not to be recommended - it is a dangerous valley to enter. It is in this respect like an affliction, which, if it troubles someone and he opposes it with the force of his patience and will, becomes a perfecter and purifier of his soul; it cooks what is raw in it and clarifies what is turbid in it. But one cannot recommend an affliction. No-one can create an affliction for himself so as to profit from these factors which prepare and train the soul; neither should he bring about an affliction for someone else on this pretext.

---

13. B. Russell: *Marriage and Morals*, London, 1976, p. 86.

Here, also, Russell has something valuable to say:

> Suffering fills people with energy, like an invaluable counterweight. Someone who deems himself to be entirely contented will not exert himself any further for happiness. But I do not advocate that this be made a pretext for causing others suffering so that they may tread a profitable path, because it often gives the opposite result and destroys man. Rather, it is better in this case to submit our own selves to chance events that fall in our way.[14]

As far as we know, the effects and advantages of afflictions and misfortunes have been much emphasized in Islamic teachings, and they are well-known as signs of God, but this in no way permits anyone to create afflictions for himself or for others on this pretext.

Moreover, there is a difference between love an affliction; and that is that love, more than any other factor, is against reason. Wherever is sets foot it ousts reason from its governing position. This is why love and reason are well-known in mystic literature as two rivals. The antagonism between the philosophers and the mystics originates from here, the former depending on, and confiding in, the power of reason, the latter in the power of love. In Sūfī literature, reason is always condemned and defeated in this field of competition. Sa'dī says:

My well-wishers advise me.
It is useless to make bricks on the sea.
But the power of yearning prevails over patience.
The pretension of the intellect over love is futile.

Another poet has said:

I drew a comparison for the counsel of reason in the path of love.
It is like a fall of dew trying to trace a pattern on the sea.

How can a force which is as powerful as this, which snatches the reins of the will out of our hands, and which, in the words of Rūmī "blows a

14. *ibid.*, Translated from the Persian, original untraced.

man here and there like a blade of straw in the hands of a fierce wind", and in the words of Russell "is something with propensity for anarchy", be recommendable?

At any rate, it is one thing to happen to have useful results, but it is another to be advisable or recommendable. From this it will be seen that the objection and complaint which some Islamic jurists have levelled against some of the Islamic philosophers[15] who have set forth this matter in their metaphysics and have explained its results and advantages, is invalid. For the former imagined that the opinion of the latter group of philosophers was that this matter is both advisable and recommendable, whereas they only considered the useful effects of this kind of love which appear under conditions of piety and chastity, without recommending or advising it, just as they would have done with afflictions or misfortunes.

* * * * *

LOVE AND DEVOTION TO THOSE CLOSE TO GOD

We have said that love is not restricted only to an animal love of a sexual or parental kind. Rather, there is another kind of love and attraction which is situated in a more rarefied atmosphere, and is completely beyond the confines of matter or materiality. It originates from an instinct far above that of the preservation of generations, and is in fact something which separates the universe of man from the universe of animals. This is spiritual, or human, love, falling in love with excellence and goodness, becoming enamoured of the virtues of man and the beauty of reality.

Those loves which are for the sake of a colour
Are not love: in the end they are a disgrace;
Since love of the dead is not enduring,
Because the dead one never comes back to us.

15. Ibn Sīnā in his *Treatise on Love* (*Risāl-e 'ishq*), and Ṣadru 'd-Dīn ash-Shīrazī in the third journey of his *Asfār al-arba'*.

(But) love of the living is every moment
Fresher than a bud in the spirit and the sight
Choose the love of that Living One Who is everlasting,
Who gives thee to drink of the wine that increases life.
Choose the love of Him from Whose love
All the prophets gained power and glory.[16]

And it is love which is mentioned in many of the verses of the Qur'ān, especially by the word "*maḥabbah*",

These verses can be placed in several groups:

1. Verses which describe the believers, and speak of the deep devotion and love they have for God or the other believers:

وَالَّذِينَ آمَنُوا أَشَدُّ حُبًّا لِلَّهِ

But those that believe love Allāh more ardently. (al-Baqarah, 2:165)

وَالَّذِينَ تَبَوَّءُوا الدَّارَ وَالْإِيمَانَ مِن قَبْلِهِمْ يُحِبُّونَ مَنْ هَاجَرَ إِلَيْهِمْ وَلَا يَجِدُونَ فِي صُدُورِهِمْ حَاجَةً مِّمَّا أُوتُوا وَيُؤْثِرُونَ عَلَىٰ أَنفُسِهِمْ وَلَوْ كَانَ بِهِمْ خَصَاصَةٌ

And those who made their dwelling in the abode, and in belief, before them, love whosoever has emigrated to them not finding in their breasts any need for what they have been given, and preferring others above themselves, even though poverty be their portion. (al-Ḥashr, 59:9)

2. Verses which speak of the love of God for believers:

إِنَّ اللَّهَ يُحِبُّ التَّوَّابِينَ وَيُحِبُّ الْمُتَطَهِّرِينَ

Truly Allāh loves those who repent, and He loves those who cleanse themselves. (al-Baqarah, 2:222)

16. Adapted from Nicholson's translation of Rūmī, *Mathnavī*, bk. 1

وَ اللهَ يُحِبُّ الْمُحْسِنِينَ

And Allāh loves the good doers. (Āl 'Imrān, 3:148 and al-Mā'idah, 5:13)

إِنَّ اللهَ يُحِبُّ الْمُتَّقِينَ

Surely Allāh loves those who guard themselves. (at-Tawbah, 9:4 and 7)

وَاللهُ يُحِبُّ الْمُطَّهِّرِينَ

And Allāh loves those who cleanse themselves. (at-Tawbah, 9:108)

إِنَّ اللهَ يُحِبُّ الْمُقْسِطِينَ

Surely Allāh loves the just. (al-Ḥujurāt, 49:9 and al-Mumtaḥinah, 60:8)

3. Verses which include two-way affections and reciprocal love: the love of God for the believers, the love of the believers for God; and the love of the believers for each other:

قُلْ إِن كُنتُمْ تُحِبُّونَ اللهَ فَاتَّبِعُونِي يُحْبِبْكُمُ اللهُ وَيَغْفِرْ لَكُمْ ذُنُوبَكُمْ

Say "if you love Allāh, follow me, and Allāh will love you, and forgive you your sins." (Āl 'Imrān, 3:31)

فَسَوْفَ يَأْتِي اللهُ بِقَوْمٍ يُحِبُّهُمْ وَيُحِبُّونَهُ

Allāh will assuredly bring a people He loves, and who love Him. (al-Mā'idah, 5:54)

إِنَّ الَّذِينَ آمَنُوا وَعَمِلُوا الصَّالِحَاتِ سَيَجْعَلُ لَهُمُ الرَّحْمَـٰنُ وُدًّا

Surely those who believe and do deeds of righteouness - unto them the All-merciful shall assign love. (Maryam, 19:96)

وَجَعَلَ بَيْنَكُم مَّوَدَّةً وَرَحْمَةً

And He has sent between you love and compassion. (ar-Rūm, 30: 21)

And it is love which Ibrāhīm wanted for his offspring,[17] and which the last Prophet also sought by the order of God for his kinsmen.[18]

From what we have been told from *ḥadīth*, the spirit and essence of religion is nothing but love. Burayd al-'Ijlī said:

> "I was in the presence of Imām al-Bāqir (a.s.), and there was a traveller from Khurāsān who had traversed that long journey on foot. He had the honour of meeting the Imām. His feet, which were showing through his shoes, were cut, and he had taken his shoes off. He said: 'By God, the only thing that brought me from whence I have come is love of you, the Household (of the Prophet).' The Imām said: 'By God, if a stone loved us, God would unite it with us, and join it to us. Is the religion other than love?'"[19]

A man said to Imām aṣ-Ṣādiq (a.s.): "We have named our children after you and your fathers; will this action be of any benefit to us?" He said: "Yes, by God; is the religion other than love?" Then he gave the verse *If you love Allāh, follow me, and Allāh will love you* as evidence.[20]

Basically, it is love which brings obedience: the lover does not have the power to refuse the wishes of the one he loves. We have seen this with our own eyes when a youth who was in love left everything when faced with his loved one, his beloved, and sacrificed everything for her.

The obedience and worship of God is in proportion to the love which man has for God, as Imām aṣ-Ṣādiq (a.s.) said: "Disobey God and show that you love Him; by my life, that is something amazing. If your love

17. Ibrāhīm, 14:37.
18. ash-Shūrā, 42:23.
19. *Safīnatu 'l-biḥār*, vol. 1, p. 102 (under *Ḥubb*).
20. *ibid.*, p. 662 (under *Samā*)

were true, you would have obeyed Him, for the lover is submissive before the one whom he loves."

* * * * *

THE POWER OF LOVE IN SOCIETY

The power of love is a great and effective force in relation to society; the best societies are those which are administered by the power of love: both the love of the leader and the ruler for the people, and the love and devotion of the people for the leader and ruler.

The feeling and love of the ruler is an important factor in the stability and longevity of a government, and until that factor exists the leader cannot, or finds it very difficult to, lead the society, train people to be law-abiding individuals, and even establish justice and egality in that society. But once he does so, people will be so lawfully minded that they will see the affection of their ruler and it is this affection which will attract them to obedience and dutifulness.

The Qur'ān addresses the Prophet and says to him that he has a great power in his hands to influence people and to administer society:

فَبِمَا رَحْمَةٍ مِّنَ اللهِ لِنتَ لَهُمْ ۖ وَلَوْ كُنتَ فَظًّا غَلِيظَ الْقَلْبِ لَانفَضُّوا مِنْ حَوْلِكَ ۖ
فَاعْفُ عَنْهُمْ وَاسْتَغْفِرْ لَهُمْ وَشَاوِرْهُمْ فِي الْأَمْرِ

It is by some mercy of Allāh that thou art gentle to them; hadst thou been harsh and hard of heart, they would have scattered from about thee. So pardon them, and pray forgiveness for them, and take counsel with them in the affair. (Āl 'Imrān, 3:159)

Here it is made clear that the cause of the people's coming to the Prophet is the affection and love which he has bestowed on them. Then it orders him to forgive them and to ask for forgiveness for them and to consult with them. These are all among the effects of love and friendship, just as tolerance, patience and forbearance are also among the degrees of love and kindness.

By the sword of clemency he ('Alī) redeemed so many throats
Of such a multitude from the sword.
The sword of clemency is sharper than the sword of iron;
Nay, it is more productive of victory than a hundred armies.[21]

The Qur'ān also says:

وَلَا تَسْتَوِي الْحَسَنَةُ وَلَا السَّيِّئَةُ ۚ ادْفَعْ بِالَّتِي هِيَ أَحْسَنُ فَإِذَا الَّذِي بَيْنَكَ وَبَيْنَهُ عَدَاوَةٌ كَأَنَّهُ وَلِيٌّ حَمِيمٌ

Not equal are the good deed and the evil deed. Repel with that which is fairer and behold, he between whom and thee there is enmity shall be as if he were a loyal friend. (Fuṣṣilat, 41:34)

Forgive, o son, that man can trap
By goodness and do savage deeds with fetters,
Chain the neck of the enemy with mercy,
Which noose no blade can cut.

In his firman to Mālik al-Ashtar, when he appointed him to the governorship of Egypt, Amīr al-mu'minīn also explained how his behaviour with the people should be:

وَأَشْعِرْ قَلْبَكَ الرَّحْمَةَ لِلرَّعِيَّةِ، وَالْمَحَبَّةَ لَهُمْ، وَاللُّطْفَ بِهِمْ... فَأَعْطِهِمْ مِنْ عَفْوِكَ وَصَفْحِكَ مِثْلَ الَّذِي تُحِبُّ أَنْ يُعْطِيَكَ اللهُ مِنْ عَفْوِهِ وَصَفْحِهِ

Awaken in your heart mercy for (your) subjects and love for them, and kindness towards them . . . So give them of your forgiveness and your pardon, just as you would like Allāh to give you of his forgiveness and pardon.[22]

21. Rūmī, bk. 1.
22. *Nahju 'l-balāghah*, Letter no. 53.

The heart of the ruler must be a focus of affection and love towards the nation; power and force are not enough. People can be driven like sheep by power and force, but their inner strengths cannot be awakened and put to use. Not only is power and force not sufficient; even justice, if it is lifelessly enforced, is not enough. Rather the ruler must love the people from his heart like a loving father, show his affection towards them and also have an attractive personality which fosters devotion, so that he may make use of their wills, their ambitions and their great human strengths in furthering his own divine aim.

* * * * *

THE BEST MEANS FOR REFINING THE SOUL

The previous discussion on the subject of love and affection was an introduction, and now we want gradually to draw a conclusion. The most important part of our discussion - it is in fact the foundation of our discussion - is whether love and affection for those near to God, and devotion to persons of excellence, is an aim in itself, or whether it is a means for refining the soul, reforming one's morals, and acquiring human virtues and excellences.

In animal love, all the interests and endeavour of the lover is towards the form of the loved one and the harmony of the loved one's limbs and the colour and beauty of the skin, and these are instincts which pull and attract man. However, after the satisfying of the instinct, these fires have no brightness, become cool, and are eventually extinguished.

But human love, as we have said, is life and vitality; it engenders obedience and loyalty. This is the love which makes the lover resemble the loved one, makes him try to be a manifestation of the loved one and a copy of the loved one's behaviour, just as Khwājah Naṣīru 'd-Dīn aṭ-Ṭūsī says in his commentary to Ibn Sīnā's *Kitābu 'l-ishārāt wa 't-tanbihāt* (Book of Directives and Remarks)

> (*The love of*) the soul is that whose source is the essential resemblance of the soul of the lover with the soul of the beloved. Most of the lover's delight is in the characteristics of the beloved which proceed from the soul of the beloved . . . It makes the soul tender, yearning and ecstatic and gives it a delicacy of feeling which detaches it from the distractions of the world.[23]

Love pushes towards similarity and resemblance, and its power causes the lover to assume the form of the beloved. Love is like an electric wire which joins the being of the be loved to the lover and transfers the qualities of the beloved to him; and it is here that the choice of a beloved is of fundamental importance. Thus Islam has given much importance to the subject of finding a friend and taking a companion. There are many verses (of the Qur'ān) and sayings (of the Prophet and the Imams) in this domain, because friendship causes resemblance, creates beauty and brings imprudence.

> *Where its shines its light it sees the defect as art, and the thorn as rose and jasmine.*[24]

---

23. *Sharḥ Kitābu 'l-ishārāt wa 't-tanbihāt*, Tehran, 1379 A.H., vol. 3, p. 383.
24. As for love, there are blemishes also. Among these is the fact that the lover, as a result of his preoccupation with the goodness of his beloved, is heedless of the beloved's defects:

حُبُّ الشَّيْءِ يُعْمِيْ وَيُصِمُّ

Love of anything brings a blindness and a deafness.

وَمَنْ عَشِقَ شَيْئاً أَعْشَى بَصَرَهُ، وَأَمْرَضَ قَلْبَهُ

Anyone who loves something, his sight becomes defective and his heart sick. (*Nahju 'l-balāghah*).

Saʿdī wrote in his *Rose Garden* (*Gulistān*):

> *For everyone it is the same, one's own mind seems perfect and one's own child beautiful.*

This bad effect is not inconsistent with what we said earlier on, i.e., that the effect ⇒

In some of the verses (of the Qur'ān) and sayings (of the Prophet and Imams) a warning is given about frequenting and befriending unwholesome and rotten people, and in some of them a call is made to pure-hearted friendship.

Ibn 'Abbās said: "We were in the presence of the Prophet when it was asked: 'Who is the best companion?' He replied: 'That person who when you see him, you are reminded of God; when he speaks, your knowledge increases; when he acts, you fall to thinking of the hereafter and the Resurrection'."[25]

⇐ of love is a sensitization of the intelligence and perception; sensitization of the intelligence means that it brings man out of slow-wittedness, and actualises his potential. However, the bad effect of love is not that it dulls man's wits but that it makes man heedless, and the question of intelligence is different from that of heedlessness. Very often, as a result of the preservation of a balance in sensibilities, dim-witted persons are less prone to heedlessness.

Love makes the understanding more keen, but the attention one-sided and one-tracked. Thus, we said before that the property of love was singleness, and it is as a result of this singleness and focality that the defect arises, and attention to other things diminishes.

What is more, not only does love cause defectiveness, but it shows the defects as something good; for one of love's effects is that wherever it shines its light, it makes that place seem beautiful, it turns one speck of goodness into the sun. It even makes black seem white and darkness light. As Vaḥshī said:

If you sat in the ball of my eye,
Naught would you see but the goodness of Laylā.

And it is perhaps for this reason that love is unlike knowledge, which is completely a function of what is known. Love's inward and psychic aspect is greater than its outward and real aspect; that is to say, the equilibrium of love is not a function of the scales of goodness, but more a function of the scales of the potentiality and essence of the lover. In fact, the lover has an essence, a matter, a latent fire which is seeking an excuse, an object. Whenever it happens to encounter an object and finds compatibility - the secret of this compatibility is still unknown, and that is why it is said that love is unreasonable - this inner potentiality manifests itself and creates goodness according to its own ability, not according to what exists in the beloved. This is what the sentence above refers to when it says that the lover sees the defect of the beloved as art and the thorn as rose and jasmine.

25. *Biḥāru 'l-anwār*, vol. 15, bk. 10, p. 51 (old edition).

Mankind is in dire need of the elexir of love for pure and virtuous people, so that love may be cultivated, and so that love for such people may create a resemblance and similarity to them in mankind.

A variety of ways have been recommended for reforming one's morals and refining the soul, and various methods have come into existence, one of which is the Socratic method. According to this, man must reform himself by way of his intellect and his own devising. A man should first of all find complete faith in the benefits of the purification of, and the harm of confusion in, the morals, and then, one by one, find the blameworthy qualities with the instrument of his intellect – like someone who wants to pick out the hairs from inside his nose one by one, or like a farmer who, by his own hand, pulls out the tares from the furrows of his land, or like someone who wants to clean his wheat of small stones and soil by his own hand – and then cleanse these bad qualities from the harvest of his being. According to this method, one must gradually remove moral depravities by patience, perseverance, careful reckoning and applied thought, and purify the gold of one's being from false coin. Perhaps it should be said that it is not possible for the intellect to acquit itself of this task.

Philosophers seek to reform morality by thought and reckoning. For example, they say that purity and continence are the cause of man's honour and character in the eyes of people, and greed and avarice are the consequences of hardship and inferiority; or they say that knowledge is the consequence of power and ability, knowledge is like this and like that, knowledge is "the seal of the kingdom of Solomon", knowledge is the light along man's path which illuminates the pitfalls in his way; or they say that envy and malevolence are spiritual sicknesses, from which evil consequences will result as far as society is concerned; and so on.

There is no doubt that this way is a correct way, and this means is a good means; but we are talking about the balance of the value of this means in comparison with any other means. Just as a car is, for example, a good means, but when it is compared to an airplane we must examine carefully the extent of its value.

First of all, we have no argument with the value of the way of the intellect as regards guidance, that is to say from the point of view of hove far so-called intellectual reasoning reveals reality in the matter of ethics, how far it is true, and in conformity with the facts, and is not faulty and erroneous. We will only say this much, that there are countless philosophical schools of ethics and education, and this problem has still not passed beyond the boundaries of discussion and argument as far as reasoning is concerned. Moreover we know that the Sūfīs are all in agreement when they say:

The leg of the reasoners is of wood;
A wooden leg is very infirm.[26]

At the moment, our discussion does not concern this aspect, instead it concerns how far this way can reach. The mystics and people of the spiritual journey have recommended the way of love and fellowship in place of following the way of the intellect and reasoning. They say that one should find a perfect being and hang the halter of love for, and fellowship with, him round one's heart, since this is both less dangerous that the way of the intellect and reasoning, and also swifter. By way of comparison, these two paths are like the old-fashioned way of doing something by hand and the way of doing it by machine. The effect of the power of love and fellowship on the doing away with moral vices from the heart is similar to the effect of chemicals on metals; for example, an etcher removes what is unwanted on his plate by the application of strong acid, not by using a nail, or the point of a knife, or anything like that. However, the effect of the intellect in reforming moral evils is like the work of someone who wants to separate iron-fillings from dust by hand; how excruciating and troublesome that would be! If he had a powerful magnet to hand, perhaps he could separate them with one sweep. The force of love and fellowship gathers the vicious qualities like

26. Rūmī, *Mathnavī*, bk. 1.

the magnet and castes them away. The mystics believe that love of, and fellowship with, purified and perfect individuals is like an automatic apparatus which gathers the vices together by itself and ejects them. If the state of being attracted finds the right object, it is one of the best states, and it is this which refines and bestows exceptional qualities.

Truly those who have taken this path want to reform their morality through the strength of love, and they have relied on the power of affection and fellowship. Experience has shown them that companionship with the pure and fellowship and love for them has affected their spirits to an extent which reading hundreds of volumes on ethics has not.

Rūmī has related the message of love by the complaint of the reed; he says:

Whoever saw a poison and antedote like the reed?
Whoever saw a sympathiser and a longing lover like the reed?
Whoever's garment is torn by love
Is entirely cleansed of covetousness or blemish.
Hail, O Love, that bringest us good gain -
O physician of all our ills.[27]

Sometimes we see some great person whose followers imitate him even in the way of walking, dressing, meeting with people and gesturing. This imitation is not voluntary, it is automatic and by the force of nature. It is the strength of love and fellowship which has influenced all the elements of the lover's existence and has made him resemble his beloved in every one of his states. This is why every human being must search for a man of reality and truth for his own reformation, and devote himself to him so that he can truly reform himself.

If there is the desire for union in your head, O Ḥāfiẓ,
You must become like clay in the craftsman's hands.

27. *ibid.*

When a man who, however much he may at first have decided to be pious and do good deeds, again falls prey to weakness in the fundamentals of his aspiration, finds love and fellowship, that weakness and lethargy will then go away, and his resolution will become firm and his ambition strong.

Love of the good ones unscrupulously took away heart and religon;
The rook in chess cannot take as much as a beautiful face can capture.
Do you imagine that Majnūn became deranged by himself?
It was the glance of Laylā that transported him among the stars.
I did not find my way alone to the source of the sun,
I was a mote, and love for you bore me up.
It was the curve of your eyebrow, it was your heavenly hand,
Which circled round in this revelry and drove my heart insane.[28]

History tells of great persons in whose spirit and soul a revolution was created by love and fellowship with a perfect one - at least according to the idea of their followers. Mawlānā Rūmī is one of such persons. He was not from the first so consumed (by love) and full of commotion. He was a scholar, and was calmly and quietly engaged in teaching in a corner of his town. But from the day that he encountered Shams-e Tabrīzī and the desire for fellowship with him seized his heart and soul his manner completely changed and a fire flared up inside him. It was like a fuse which has fallen into a gunpowder store and bursts into flames. He was, apparently, a follower of Ash'arism, but his *Mathnavī* is without doubt one of the greatest books in the world. All the poetry of this man is surging, in movement. He composed the *Dīwān of Shams* in memory of his desire, his beloved; and in the *Mathnavī* too, he mentions him a great deal. We see Mawlānā Rūmī in the *Mathnavī* searching after something, but as soon as he remembers Shams a wild storm brews up in his spirit, and roaring waves surge up in him; he says:

At this moment my soul has plucked my skirt,
He has caught the perfume of Joseph's vest.

28. 'Allāmah Ṭabā'ṭabā'ī.

(He said:) "For the sake of our years of companionship,
Recount one of those sweet ecstasies,
That earth and heaven may laugh,
That intellect and spirit and eye may increase a hundredfold,"
I said: "The one who is far from his beloved is
Like an invalid who is far from the doctor.
How should I describe (not a vein of mine is sensible)
That Friend who hath no peer.
The description of this severance and this heart's blood
Do thou at present leave over till another time.
Do not seek trouble and turmoil and bloodshed:
Say no more concerning Shams-e Tabrīzī."[29]

And this is the fitting meaning of what Ḥāfiẓ said:

The nightingale learnt its song by the favour of the
rose, otherwise there would not have been
Any of this song and music fashioned from its beak.

From this we can infer that exertion and being drawn, or action and attraction must go together. Nothing can be accomplished from effort without attraction, just as being drawn where there is no effort will not reach its aim.

* * * * *

EXAMPLES FROM THE HISTORY OF ISLAM

In the history of Islam we find distinguished and unprecedented examples of the strong love and devotion of Muslims for the person of the Prophet. In fact, one difference between the 'school' of the prophets and the 'school' of the philosophers is just this, that the pupils of philosophers are just students, and philosophers have no more influence than that of a teacher; but the influence of the prophets is like

29. Adapted from Nicholson's translation of Rūmī, *Mathnavī*, bk. 1

the influence of someone, a beloved, who has entered into the depths of the spirit of the lover, caught him in his grasp, and taken a hold on every element of his life.

* * * * *

One of those who dearly loved the Prophet was Abū Dharr al-Ghifārī. The Prophet had given the order to march to Tabūk (a hundred farsangs - about four hundred miles - north of Medina, close to the border with Syria). Some made excuses, the hypocrites tried to disrupt things, but eventually a powerful army set out. They had no military equipment, and they were in difficulties and in need as regards food too, so that sometimes some of them would make do with a single date; however they were all full of vigour and cheerful. Love created their strength and the force of attraction of the Prophet gave them their power.

Abū Dharr was also marching towards Tabūk with this army. On the way three persons, one after the other, fell behind, and the Prophet was informed about each one as he dropped back. Each time he said:

> If there is any good in him, God will make him come back;
> and if there is no good in him, it is better that he go.

The thin, weak camel of Abū Dharr fell back, and then Abū Dharr was also seen to be behind. "O Messenger of Allāh! Abū Dharr has fallen back too!' Then the Prophet repeated the same sentence:

> If there is any good in him, God will make him come back;
> and if there is no good in him, it is better that he go.

The army then continued on its way and Abū Dharr stayed behind; but there was nothing to be done - his animal stayed in the same state. No matter what he did, it would not move, and he had now dropped several miles behind. He set the camel free and took the pack on his own shoulder, and in the hot weather he set out over the scorching sand. He was thirsty and it was killing him. He came across some rocks in the shade of a hill and among them some rainwater had gathered, but he said to himself that he would never drink until his friend, the Prophet of Allāh, had drunk. He filled his water-skin, slung it also on his back, and hastened off in the direction of the Muslims.

In the distance they espied a figure. "O Messenger of Allāh! We have seen a distant figure coming towards us!"

He said that it had to be Abū Dharr. He came nearer — yes, it was Abū Dharr, but exhaustion and thirst took his feet away from under him. He was afraid he would collapse. The Prophet said to give him some water quickly, but he said with a feeble voice that he had water with him. The Prophet said:

"You have water, but you are near to dying from thirst!"

"Yes, O Messenger of Allāh! When I tasted the water I refused to drink any before my friend, the Messenger of Allāh."[30]

In all truth, in which of the world's religions can we find such a state of captivation, such restlessness and such unselfishness?

* * * * *

Another of these enamoured and selfless people was Bilāl al-Ḥabashī. The Quraysh were subjecting him to insupportable torture in Mecca, and they were tormenting him under the burning sun by laying him on scorching stones. They wanted from him that he say the names of the idols and declare his belief in them, and that he renounce, and say he would have nothing to do with, Muḥammad. In the sixth part of the *Mathnawī*, Rūmī has related the agonising story of Bilāl, and he has justly made a masterpiece out of it. He says: Abū Bakr consElled him to hide his belief, but he did not have the fortitude for dissimulation for "love was ever rebellious and deadly."

30. *Biḥāru 'l-anwār*, vol. 21, pp. 215-216 (new ed.).

Bilāl was devoting his body to the thorns.
His master was flogging him by way of correction,
(Saying:) "Why dost thou celebrate Aḥmad?
Wicked slave, thou disbelievest in my religion!"
He was beating him in the sun with thorns
(While) he cried vauntingly "One!"
Till when Ṣiddīq (Abū Bakr) was passing in that neighbourhood,
Those cries of "One!" reached his ears.
Afterwards he saw him in private and admonished him:
"Keep thy belief hidden from the Jews.
He (God) knows (all) secrets: conceal thy desire."
He (Bilāl) said: "I repent before thee, O prince."
There was much repenting of this sort,
(Till) at last he became quit of repenting,
And proclaimed and yielded up his body to tribulation,
Crying: "O Muḥammad! O enemy of vows and repentance!
O thou with whom my body and all my veins are filled!
How should there be room therein for repentance?
Henceforth I will banish repentance from this heart.
How should I repent of the life everlasting?"
Love is the All-subduer, and I am subdued by Love:
By Love's blindness I have been made bright like the sun.
O fierce wind, before Thee I am a straw:
How can I know where I shall fall?
Whether I am Bilāl or the new moon,
I am running on and following the course of Thy sun.
What has the moon to do with stoutness or thinness?
She runs at the heels of the sun, like a shadow.
The lovers have fallen into a fierce-torrent:
They have set their hearts on the ordinance of Love.
(They are) like the millstone turning round and round
Day and night and moaning incessantly.[31]

* * * * *

31. Adapted from Nicholson's translation of Rūmī, *Mathnavī*, bk. 1.

Islamic historians have given the names of the Raid of ar-Rajīʿ and the Day of ar-Rajīʿ respectively to a famous historical event and the day on which it occurred, and there is an interesting and fascinating story attached to it.

A group from the ʿAḍal and al-Qārah tribes who were apparently from the same ancestral stock as the Quraysh and who dwelt in the proximity of Mecca came to the Messenger of Allāh in the third year of the Hijrah and said: "Some people from our tribe have chosen Islam, so send a group of Muslims to us that they may instruct us in the meaning of the religion, teach us the Qur'ān and inform us of the principles and laws of Islam."

The Messenger of Allāh sent six of his companions along with them for this purpose, and he entrusted the leadership of this group to a man called Marthad ibn Abī Marthad al-Ghanawī, or else to a man called ʿAṣim ibn Thābit ibn Abi 'l-Aqlaḥ.

The envoys of the Messenger set out in the company of this mission that had come to Medina, till they reached the area which was where the Hadhīl tribe lived, and there they halted.[32] The friends of the Messenger had settled down to sleep without leaving anything from any where, when all at once a group from the Hudhayl tribe fell upon them like a thunderbolt with their swords drawn. It became clear that the mission that had come to Medina had either had the intention of acting deceitfully from the beginning, or else had become despondent on reaching this place and had had a change of heart. At any rate, it is known that these people sided with the Hudhayl tribe with the aim of seizing these six envoys. As soon as the friends of the Messenger were aware of what was happening, they swiftly dashed for their arms, and got ready to defend themselves, but the Hudhaylī swore that they did not intend to kill them. They wanted to deliver them to the Quraysh in Mecca and get something for them, and they were prepared to make a pact with them there and then that they would not kill them. Three of

32. At a place called ar-Rajīʿ. (tr.)

these men including 'Aṣim ibn Thābit said that would not accept the shame of a pact with polytheists, and fought until they were killed. But the three other men by the names of Zayd ibn ad-Dathinnah ibn Mu'āwiyah, Khubayb ibn 'Adīy and 'Abdullāh ibn Ṭāriq showed themselves more flexible and surrrendered.

The Hudhaylī bound these three men firmly with cord and set out towards Mecca. Near Mecca, 'Abdullāh ibn Ṭāriq managed to get his hand free of the bonds and reach for his sword, but the enemy did not let him take the opportunity and killed him by hurling stones. Zayd and Khubayb were carried to Mecca, and they traded them in exchange for two captives from the Hudhayl who were held in Mecca, and then they went away.

Ṣafwān ibn Umayyah al-Qurashī bought Zayd from the person to whom he belonged so as to kill him to avenge the blood of his father who had been killed in Uḥud (or Badr). To kill him he took him outside Mecca. The people of the Quraysh assembled to see what would happen, and they brought Zayd to his place of execution. He came forward with his courageous gait and did not tremble even the slightest in his walking. Abū Sufyān was one of the spectators, and he thought he would take advantage of the circumstances of the last moments of Zayd's life: perhaps he could get a statement of contrition and remorse or an avowal of hatred of the Messenger from him. He stepped forward and said to Zayd:

> "I adjure you by God, Zayd, don't you wish that Muḥammad was with us now in your place so that we might cut off his head, and that you were with your family?"

"By God". said Zayd, "I don't wish that Muḥammad now were in the place he occupies and that a thorn could hurt him, and that I were sitting with my family."

Abū Sufyān's mouth stood agape with surprise. He turned to the other

Quraysh and said:

> "By God, I swear I have never seen a man who was so loved as Muḥammad's companions love him."

After a while, Khubayb ibn 'Adīy's turn fell, and he too was taken outside Mecca for execution. There he requested the assembly to let him pray two *rak'ah* of prayer. They agreed, and he recited the prayers in all humility, respect and absorbtion. Then he spoke to the crowd, and said:

> "I swear by God that were it not that you would think that I only delayed out of fear of death, I would have prolonged my prayer."

They condemned Khubayb to crucifixion; and it was then that the sweet voice of Khubayb ibn 'Adīy was heard, with a perfect spirituality which held everyone in its spell and caused some to caste themselves down on the earth in fear, entreating God with these words:

اَللّٰهُمَّ إِنَّا قَدْ بَلَّغْنَا رِسَالَةَ رَسُولِكَ، فَبَلِّغْهُ الغَداةَ مَا يُصْنَعُ بِنَا، اَللّٰهُمَّ أَحْصِهِمْ عَدَدًا، وَاقْتُلْهُمْ بَدَدًا، وَلاَ تُغَادِرْ مِنْهُمْ أَحَدًا.

O God! We have delivered the message of Thy Messenger; so tell him tomorrow what has been done to us. O God! Reckon them by number and kill them one by one, let none of them remain.[33]

* * * * *

As we know, the incident of Uḥud ended in a sorrowful way for the Muslims. Seventy Muslims were martyred, including Ḥamzah, the paternal uncle of the Prophet. The Muslims were winning at the beginning, but later, as a result of the lack of discipline of a group who were placed atop a hill by the Prophet, the Muslims were subject to a surprise attack by the enemy. One group were killed, another group was scattered, while the small group round the Prophet remained. The only thing this reduced group could do was to gather their forces once again

33. Ibn Isḥāq's *The Life of Muhammad*, translation of A. Guillaume, London, 1955, pp. 426-428.

and become an obstacle to the further advance of the enemy, especially when the rumour that the Prophet had been killed was a further cause for the scattering of the Muslims. But as soon as they heard that the Prophet was still alive, their spirits returned to them.

A number of wounded had fallen on the ground and they did not at all know what their fate would be. One of the wounded was Saʿd ibn ar-Rabīʿ, and he had received twelve mortal wounds. In the middle of all this one of the escaping Muslims reached Saʿd, when he had fallen on the ground, and told him that he had heard the Prophet had been killed. Saʿd said:

> Even if Muḥammad has been killed, the God of Muḥammad has not; the religion of Muḥammad remains too. Why do you not stay and defend your religion?

Away from this, after the Prophet had collected and verified his companions, he counted them one by one to see who had been killed and who was still alive. He did not find Saʿd ibn ar-Rabīʿ, so he asked who would go to find out what had really happened to Saʿd for him. One of the Anṣār said he was ready. When the Anṣār found that Saʿd was at his last breath, he said to him: "O Saʿd! The Prophet has sent me to find out for him whether you are alive or dead."

"Give my greeting to the Prophet," said Saʿd, "and say that Saʿd is a dead man, for no more than a few breaths are left of his life. Tell the Prophet that Saʿd said: 'May God reward you by us better than he has rewarded any prophet by his people'."

Then he spoke to the Anṣār and told him: "Convey a message too from me to my brothers of the Anṣār and the other companions of the Prophet. Tell them that Saʿd said: 'You have no excuse with God if anything has happened to your Prophet while you can flutter an eyelid'."[34]

* * * * *

34. *Sharḥ* of Ibn Abi 'l-Ḥadīd, Beirut, vo1. 3, p. 574; and *ibid.* (note 33) p. 387.

The pages of the early history of Islam are full of such acts of devotion, deeds of love and episodes of beauty. In all the history of mankind, no-one can be found who was loved so much as the Messenger, and the object of so much affection from his friends, companions, wives and children, who loved him so deeply and sincerely.

Ibn Abi 'l-Ḥadīd writes in his *Sharḥ* (commentary on) *Nahju 'l-balāghah*:

> "No-one heard him (the Messenger) speak without love for him taking a place in his heart, and without becoming inclined to him. Thus the Quraysh called the Muslims round Mecca "*ṣubāt*" (the infatuated ones) and said: 'The fear is that al-Walīd ibn al-Mughīrah give his heart to the religion of Muḥammad; and if Walīd, who is the cream of the Quraysh give his heart, all the Quraysh will pledge their hearts to it.'
>
> They also said: 'His speech is magic, it inebriates more than wine.' They forbade their sons to sit with him in case they might be attracted by his speech and the pull of his countenance. Whenever the Prophet sat down beside the Ka'bah near the Stone of Ismā'īl and recited the Qur'ān in a loud voice, or fell to remembering God, they would stick their fingers firmly in their ears so as not to hear and so that they would not fall under the spell of his speech and be "bewitched" by him. They gathered their garments over their heads and covered their faces so that his attractive appearance would not draw them. Nevertheless, most people believed in Islam just by hearing him once or seeing his face and his appearance and tasting the sweetness of his words."[35]

Of all the facts of Islamic history which should cause the amazement of every authropologist or sociologist, reader or researcher, is the revolution which Islam created among the pre-Islamic Arabs. By any ordinary reckoning and with the usual devices of education and training, the reform of such a society should have required the passage of much

35. *ibid.*, vo1. 2, p. 220.

time so that the old generation habituated to vice could have been extinguished and the foundations of a new generation laid afresh; but the effect of the power of attraction must not be neglected, for we said that like tongues of fire it burns away the roots of evil.

The majority of the companions of the Messenger were deeply enamoured of this great man, and it was by riding on the steed of love that such a long way was covered in such a small time, and that in a short period his community became completely changed.

The wings of my flight became the noose of love for him.
Dragging me all the way to his mountain.
How can I have a lamp before me or behind
When the light of' my beloved is not before me or behind?
His light shines on the right, on the left, above and below.
It is on my head and round my neck like a crown and a yoke.[36]

* * * * *

LOVE FOR 'ALĪ IN THE QUR'ĀN AND *SUNNAH*

What we have said so far has shed light on the value and influence of love, and it has incidentally become clear that love for the pure ones is a means for the reform and refinement of the soul, not that it is an end in itself. Now we must see whether Islam and the Qur'ān have chosen someone we should love or not. When the Qur'ān relates what the previous prophets have said, it points out that they have all said: "we do not ask a wage from people, our only reward is from God." However it addresses the Seal of the Prophets thus:

قُل لَّا أَسْأَلُكُمْ عَلَيْهِ أَجْرًا إِلَّا الْمَوَدَّةَ فِي الْقُرْبَىٰ

Say: "I do not ask of you a wage for this, except love for (my) relatives." (ash-Shūrā, 42: 23)

36. Rūmī, *Mathnavī*, bk. 1.

Here there is a need to ask why the rest of the prophets looked for no wage but the most noble Prophet asked for one for his message; why did he want friendship for his near relatives as a requital for his message?

The Qur'ān itself provides an answer to this question:

قُلْ مَا سَأَلْتُكُم مِّنْ أَجْرٍ فَهُوَ لَكُمْ ۖ إِنْ أَجْرِيَ إِلَّا عَلَى اللَّهِ ۖ وَهُوَ عَلَىٰ كُلِّ شَيْءٍ شَهِيدٌ

> *Say: "I have asked no wage of you; that shall be yours. My wage falls only upon God."* (Sabā', 34:47)

That is to say, that which I ask for as a wage accrues to you, not to me; this friendship is a halter for your own perfection and reformation, and it is called a wage. Other wise it is in fact another good which I recommend to you from the point of view that the Household and relatives of the Prophet are people who do not gather round defilement, and whose hems are clean and pure.

Love and devotion to these people brings no other result apart from obedience to the truth and adherence to virtues, and it is friendship for them which transmutes and perfects like the elexir.

Whatever the meaning of "relatives" may be, it is certain that the most obvious person to whom it is applicable is 'Alī. Imām Fakhru 'd-Dīn ar-Rāzī says:

> "Zamakhsharī relates in his (Qur'ānic exegesis) *al-Kashshāf*: 'When this verse was sent down they said: "O Messenger of Allāh! Who are the relatives to whom our love is due?" He said: "'Alī and Fāṭimah and their sons".'
>
> "It is thus established from this tradition that these four persons are "relatives" of the Prophet, and that they should enjoy the respect and love of the people, and this matter can be reasoned out in a number of ways:

1. The verse: *except love for my relatives.*
2. There is no doubt that the Prophet dearly loved Fāṭimah, and he said: "Fāṭimah is a part of my body; what harms her harms me." he also loved 'Alī and the Ḥasanayn (Ḥasan and Ḥusayn), since a great number of *mutawātir* traditions (those which are narrated by so many as to make doubt impossible) have reached us on this subject. Thus friendship of them is obligatory on all the community,[37] because the Qur'ān commands:

وَاتَّبِعُوهُ لَعَلَّكُمْ تَهْتَدُونَ

And follow him (the Prophet), hoply you will be guided. (al-A'rāf, 7:158)

"It also commands:

لَقَدْ كَانَ لَكُمْ فِي رَسُولِ اللهِ أُسْوَةٌ حَسَنَةٌ

You have a good example in Allāh's Messenger. (al-Aḥzāb, 33:21)

"These (considerations) prove that love for the Family of Muḥammad - who are 'Alī, Fāṭimah and the Ḥasanayn - is obligatory on all Muslims."[38]

There are also many traditions from the Prophet concerning love and friendship for 'Alī:

1. Ibn al-Athīr narrates that the Prophet spoke to 'Alī and said: "O 'Alī, God has embellished you with things, no dearer embellishment than which exists before his slaves: resignation from the world has been appointed for you in such a way that neither do you profit from the world, nor it from you. On you has been bestowed the love of the wretched; they are proud of your leadership, and you also of their following you. Content is he who loves you, and is a true friend to

37. The love of the Prophet towards them had no personal aspect, that is, it was not only because, for example, they were his children and grandchildren and if someone else had been in their place he would have loved them. The Prophet loved them because they were exemplary persons and God loved them, for the Prophet had other children whom he did not love to this extent and to whom his community had no such obligation.
38. *at-Tafsīru 'l-kabīr*, vol. 27, p. 166 (Egyptian ed.).

you. And woe betide he who shows enmity towards you, and lies about you."[39]

2. as-Suyūṭī relates that the Prophet said: "Love of 'Alī is faith, and enmity towards him is sedition."[40]

3. Abū Na'īm narrates that the Prophet addressed the Anṣār and said: "Shall I guide you to something which, if you grasp it after me, you will never go astray?" They said: "Yes, O Messenger of Allāh!" He said: "It is 'Alī: love him with the love (you have) for me, and respect him with the respect (you have) for me. For God has ordered me through Gabriel to tell you this."[41]

The Sunnīs have also narrated traditions from the Prophet in which observing 'Alī's face and talking of his virtues is counted as a form of worship.

1. Muḥibb aṭ-Ṭabarī narrates from 'Ā'ishah that she said: "I saw my father (Abū Bakr) gazing often at 'Alī's face. I said: 'O my father! I see you gazing often at 'Alī's face.' He said: 'O my daughter! I heard the Prophet say: Looking at the face of 'Alī is worship'."[42]

2. Ibn Ḥajar narrates from 'Ā'ishah that the Prophet said: "The best of my brothers is 'Alī, the best of my paternal uncles is Ḥamzah, and remembrance of 'Alī and speaking about him is worship."[43]

39. *Usdu 'l-ghābah*, vo1. 4, p. 23.
40. *Kanzu 'l-'ummāl.* In as-Suyūṭī, *Jam'u 'l-jawāmi'*, vol. 6, p. 156.
41. *Ḥilyatu 'l-awliyā'*, vol. 1, p. 63. There are many traditions on this subject, and we have come across more than ninety in authoritative Sunnī texts, all of which concerns love for Amīr al-mu'minīn. There also exist many traditions in Shī'ah texts, and the respected scholar al-Majlisī has gathered them together in vo1. 39 (of the new edition) of *Biḥāru 'l-anwār* in the chapter on love and hatred for Amīr al-mu'minīn; he related 123 traditions in this chapter.
42. *ar-Riyāḍu 'n-naḍirah*, vol. 2, p. 219; and about another twenty traditions, as far as we are aware, have beeen related in Sunnī texts on this subject.
43. *aṣ-Ṣawā'iqu 'l-muḥriqah*, p. 74; and five more traditions have been related in Sunnī texts on this subject.

'Alī was the most loved person before God and the Prophet, and thus naturally the best of those who are loved. Anas ibn Mālik says: "Every day, one of the children of the Anṣār would do some task for the Prophet. One day my turn came. Umm Ayman brought a chicken dish before the Prophet and said: 'Messenger of Allāh! I have caught this chicken myself and cooked it for you.' He said: 'O God! Send the best of (Thy) slaves that he may share with me in eating this chicken.' At that very moment someone knocked on the door and the Prophet said to me: 'Anas! Open the door.' I said: 'May God make it a man of the Anṣār!' But I found 'Alī in front of the door, and I said: 'The Prophet is busy.' Then I returned to stand in my place. Again there was a knock at the door, and the Prophet said: 'Open the door.' Again I prayed that it would be someone from the Anṣār. I opened the door and again it was 'Alī. I said: 'The Prophet is busy.' Then I returned to stand in my place. Yet again there was a knock at the door, and the Prophet said: 'Anas, go and open the door, and bring him in. You are not the first person to love your own people; that is not one of the Anṣār.' I went and brought 'Alī in, and he ate the chicken dish with the Prophet."[44]

* * * * *

THE SECRET OF 'ALĪ'S FORCE OF ATTRACTION

What is the reason for the friendship and love for 'Alī in people's hearts? Nobody has yet discovered the secret of this love, that is, no-one has been able to formulate it, and say that if it were like this then that would follow, or if it were like that then this would happen. However it does of course have a secret. There is something in the love which dazzles the one who loves and draws him towards it. This attraction and love are the highest degrees of love; 'Alī is the one whom people's hearts adore, whom humanity loves. Why? In what does 'Alī's extraordinariness lie, that it incites love and draws hearts towards itself, that it plays the tune

44. *al-Mustadrak 'alā aṣ-Ṣaḥīḥayn*, vol. 3, p. 131. This story is related in various ways in more than eighty narrations in authoritative Sunnī texts.

of eternal life and lives for ever? Why do all hearts find out about themselves through him, and do not feel him to be dead but find him living?

Certainly the basis for love for him is not his body, because his body is not now among us and we have not perceived it with our senses. Love for 'Alī is also not hero worship, which exists in every nation. It is a mistake, too, to say the love for 'Alī is by way of love for moral and human excellence, and that love for 'Alī is a humanistic love. It is true that 'Alī was the manifestation of the perfect man, and it is true that man loves great figures of humanity; but if 'Alī had had all those human excellences that he had - that wisdom and knowledge, that self-sacrifice and altruism, that humility and modesty, that courtesy, that kindness and mercy, that protection of the weak, that justness, that liberality and love of freedom, that respect for humanity, that generosity, that bravery, that magnanimity and mercy towards his enemies, and, in the words of Rūmī:

In bravery you are the Lion of the Lord,
*In generosity who indeed knows who you are?*45[45]

that munificence, benevolence and beneficence - if 'Alī had had all these, which he did have, but had not had the divine touch in him, it is quite certain that there would not have been the feeling of sympathy and awakening of love that there is today.

Alī is loved in the sense that he had the divine link; our hearts are unconsciously completely involved with, and connected to, the Truth, right in their depths, and since they find 'Alī to be a great sign of the Truth and a manifestation of the attributes of the Truth they are in love with him. In reality, the basis for the love for 'Alī is the connection of our souls with the Truth which has been laid in our primordial natures, and since our primordial natures are eternal, love for 'Alī is also eternal.

There are many outstanding features in 'Alī's being, but that which has

45. Rūmī, *Mathnavī*, bk. 1 (translated by Nicholson).

assigned him a resplendent and shining place for ever is his faith and morality, and it is that which has given him his divine charisma.

Sawdah al-Hamdāniyah, a self-sacrificing and devoted follower of ʿAlī, extolled ʿAlī in front of Muʿāwiyah and among other things said this verse:

May the blessing of God be vouched to him
Whom the grave took away and with whom justice was interred.
He had a pact with God that He should put no substitute in his place,
Thus he was joined with Truth and Faith.

Ṣaʿṣaʿah ibn Ṣūḥān al-ʿAbdī was another one of those lovers of ʿAlī. He was one of those who took part on that night with a few others in the burial of ʿAlī. After they had buried ʿAlī and covered his corpse with soil, Ṣaʿṣaʿah put one of his hands over his heart, threw earth over his head and said:

"May death be agreeable to you, whose birth was pure, whose patience was firm, whose holy struggle was great! You attained your aim and your commerce was fruitful.

"You fell down before your Creator, and He gladly accepted you and His angels appeared around you. You were placed near the Prophet, and God gave you a place near him. You reached the degree of your brother, Muṣṭafā, and you drank from his overflowing cup.

"I beseach God that I may follow you and that I may act according to your ways; that I may love those who love you, and be the enemy of those who are your enemy, that I may be gathered in the pavilion of your friends.

"You saw what others did not see, and reached what others did not reach; you pursued the holy struggle beside your brother, the Prophet, and you rose up for the religion of God as was worthy of it, till age-old habits were done away with, confusion curbed and Islam and the faith put in order. May the best of blessings be upon you!

"Through you the backs of the believers were made firm, the ways made clear and habits broken. No-one could amass your virtues and excellences in himself. You answered the call of the Prophet; you jumped ahead of others in accepting him: you hurried to help him, and protected him with your life. You struck with your sword, Dhu 'l-fiqār, in places of fear and savagery, and you broke the back of oppression. You caste down the structures of polytheism and vileness, and you pulled down those who were astray into dust and blood. So may you be well pleased, O Amīr al-mu'minīn!

"You were the closest of men to the Prophet, you were the first person to follow Islam. You were overflowing with certainty, strong of heart and more self-sacrificing than any, your share in good was greater. May God not deprive us of retribution for your suffering, and may He not despise us after you have gone!

"By God, I swear that your life was the key to good, the lock against exil; and your death is the key to every evil and the lock against every good. If the people had accepted you, blessings would have showered on them from the heaven and the earth; but they preferred this world to the next."[46]

Truly they preferred this world, and as a consequence they could not endure the justice and unwaveringness of 'Alī. In the end the hand of stiffness and stagnation came out of the sleeve of the people and martyred 'Alī.

'Alī - may peace be upon him - is without equal in having totally selfless friends and people who loved him, who have given their lives in the path

46. *Biḥāru 'l-anwār*, vo1. 42, pp. 295-296 (new ed.)

of friendship and love for him. Their wonderful, absorbing and stunning biographies honour the pages of Islamic history. The criminal hands of such despicable people as Ziyād ibn Abīh and his son ʻAbdullāh, as Ḥajjāj ibn Yūsuf and Mutawakkil, and at the head of them all Muʻāwiyah ibn Abī Sufyān, are stained with the blood of these human lives up to their elbows.

* * * * *

Part Two : The Power of Repulsion in ʻAlī

HOW ʻALĪ MADE ENEMIES

We shall restrict our discussion to the period of his somewhat more than four-year caliphate. ʻAlī was all the time a two-powered personality; ʻAlī always had the powers both of attraction and repulsion. In fact, we see right from the beginning of the Islamic age one group who gravitated more round ʻAlī, and another group who did not have such a good connection with him and who were occasionally pained by his existence.

But the period of ʻAlī's caliphate, and similarly the times after his death, that is to say the period of the appearance of the "history" of ʻAlī, were the age of the greater manifestation of attraction to, and repulsion from, him; to the same extent as before the caliphate his links with the society were fewer, and also his attraction and repulsion less.

ʻAlī was a man who made enemies and gave people displeasure, and this, too, is another one of his great glories. Every principled man who has an aim and struggles towards it, particularly the revolutionary who pursues the putting into practice of his sacred goals and who is referred to by the words of Allāh:

يُجَاهِدُونَ فِي سَبِيلِ اللهِ وَلَا يَخَافُونَ لَوْمَةَ لَائِمٍ

> *Who struggle in the way of Allāh, not fearing the reproach of any reproacher.* (al-Mā'idah, 5:54)

makes enemies and leaves dissatisfied people. So if his enemies did not number more than his friends, especially in his own times, they were no fewer and nor are they now.

If ʻAlī's personality were not distorted today, but were presented just as it was, many of those who pretend to be his friends would take a stand alongside his enemies.

The Prophet sent ʻAlī as a commander of an army to the Yemen. On his return he set out for Mecca to meet the Prophet, and, on reaching the environs of Mecca, he appointed one of the soldiers in his place and himself hurried on to present the account of his expedition to the Messenger of Allāh. That person divided up the garments which 'Alī had brought along with them among the soldiers, so that they could enter Mecca in new clothes. When 'Alī returned, he objected to this action, and reproved that man for lack of discipline, because no decision should have been taken about the garments before orders had been received from the Prophet about what to do with them. In the eyes of 'Alī, such an action was in fact a kind of expropriation from the *baytu 'l-māl* (the Treasury of the Muslims) without giving notification to, and obtaining permission from, the leader of the Muslims. For this reason 'Alī gave the order that they should take off the garments and put them in a particular place, until they could be delivered to the Prophet and he himself could make a decision about them. Because of this, 'Alī's soldiers became disgruntled, and, as soon as they had gone in to see the Prophet, they complained about 'Alī's harshness over the garments. The Prophet addressed them, and said:

أَيُّهَا النَّاسُ، لاَ تَشْكُوا عَلِيّاً، فَوَاللهِ إِنَّهُ لَأَخْشَنُ فِي ذَاتِ اللهِ مِنْ أَنْ يُشْكَى

> *Oh men, do not grumble about 'Alī. I swear by Allāh that he is more intensely in the way of God than that anyone should complain about him.*[1]

'Alī had no concern for anyone in the way of God. Rather, if he showed interest in someone or was concerned about him, it was because of God. Naturally, such an attitude makes enemies, and it causes offence to souls full of greed and craving and brings them pain.

None of the companions of the Prophet had devoted friends like 'Alī did, just as no-one had such bold and dangerous enemies as he did. He was someone who, even after his death, had his corpse attacked by enemies. He was himself aware of this and foresaw these things, and so he left as his will that his grave should be hidden and unknown to all but his sons, until after about a century had passed and the Umayyids had been

1. See Ibn Isḥāq, *The Life of Muhammad* (transl., A. Guillaume).

overthrown, the Khawārij overthrown too, or made all but impotent, and vendettas and avengers had become few, and Imām aṣ-Ṣādiq indicated the sacred soil of his resting place.

* * * * *

THE *NĀKITHŪN*, THE *QĀSIṬŪN* AND THE *MĀRIQŪN*

In the period of his caliphate, 'Alī expelled three groups from beside him and rose up to do battle with them: the people of (the battle of) Jamal, whom he himself named the *Nākithūn* (those who break their allegiance); the people of (the battle of) Ṣiffīn, whom he called *Qāsiṭūn* (those who deviate); and the people of (the battle of) Nahrawān, the Khawārij, whom he called the *Māriqūn* (those who miss the truth of the religion).[2]

'Alī said:

فَلَمَّا نَهَضْتُ بِالْأَمْرِ نَكَثَتْ طَائِفَةٌ، وَمَرَقَتْ أُخْرَى، وَقَسَطَ آخَرُوْنَ

When I took up the reins of government one party broke their allegiance (nakathah), another missed the truth of the religion (maraqah), and another deviated (qasaṭah).[3]

The *Nākithūn* were of a money-worshipping mentality, people of covetousness and displayers of prejudice. 'Alī's speeches about justice and equality were more for the attention of this group.

However the mind of the *Qāsiṭūn* belonged to politics, deception and sedition; they killed so as to take the reins of government into their own

2. Before 'Alī, the Prophet called these people by these names when he said to him: "After me, you will fight with the *nākithūn*, the qāsiṭūn and the māriqūn." This tradition is narrated by Ibn Abi 'l-Ḥadīd in his commentary on *Nahju 'l-balāghah* (vol. 1, p. 201), where he says that it is one of the proofs of the prophethood of Muḥammad since the tradition is quite explicit about the future and the unknown (*ghayb*), and there is no kind of hidden interpretation or ellipsis in it.
3. *Nahju 'l-balāghah* - Sermon 3 "ash- Shiqshiqīyah".

hands, and to topple the basis of 'Alī's government and his governorship. Some people advised him to come to a compromise with them and to give them, to a certain extent, what they were after, but he did not accept because he was not a person to do this kind of thing. He was ready to fight injustice, not to give his signature to it. On the one hand, Mu'āwiyah and his clique were against the basis of 'Alī's government, and then the *Qāsiṭūn* wanted to occupy the seat of the caliphate of Islam themselves. In reality 'Alī's war with them was a war with sedition and double-dealing.

The third group, which was the *Māriqūn*, had a spirit of inadmissible fanaticism, sanctimoniousness and dangerous ignorance. In relation to all these people, 'Alī was a powerful repeller and they lived in a state of non-conciliation.

One of the manifestations of 'Alī's completeness and his being a perfect individual was that, when it was called for, he faced the various factions and deviations and fought against all of them. Sometimes we see him on the scene, fighting with those who were devoted to money or to this world, and sometimes too on the scene fighting with professional politicians of the most hypocritical type, and sometimes with ignorant and deviationist men of false piety.

Our discussion is oriented towards the last group, the Khawārij. Although they have been overthrown and are no more, they present an instructive and admonitory little history. Their thinking has taken root among the Muslims, and consequently their spirit has always existed, and still does, in the shape of sanctimonious persons, all the way down these fourteen centuries, even though the individual Khawārij and even their name have disappeared, and they can be counted as a grave hindrance to the advancement of Islam and the Muslims.

* * * * *

HOW THE KHAWĀRIJ CAME INTO EXISTENCE

The word *khawārij*, that is, "rebels", comes from *khurūj*[4] which means "revolt" and "insurrection". This group came into being during the process of arbitration. The battle of Ṣiffīn, in its last day of fighting, was turning out in 'Alī's favour; Mu'āwiyah, in consultation with 'Amr ibn al-'Āṣ, conceived a skilful stratagem. He had seen that all his pains had produced no result, and that he was only one step away from defeat. He saw that there was no way to save himself except by having recourse to the creation of confusion, so he ordered that Qur'āns should be raised up on the points of spears to show that they were people of prayer and the Qur'ān, and that the Book should be used to arbitrate between the two sides. It was not the first time that this had been done, for it was the same

4. If the word *khurūj* is used with an indirect object introduced by *'alā*, it has two meanings which are near to one another. One is to stand up in a position for battle or war, and the other is disobedience, insubordination and revolt. The Arabic dictionary *al-Munjid* says that *kharaja* with an indirect object introduced by *'alā* means to come forward to fight someone, or it can be used for subjects rebelling against the king: insurrection.

The word *khawārij*, meaning revolt, comes from *khurūj* in the second sense. That group which evidence the command of 'Alī and rebelled against him is called the *khawārij*. Since they based their disobedience on a belief and on a religious ideology, they became a sect, and the name came to be used especially for them; and so it was not used for any other people who rose up after them and rebelled against the ruler of their times. If they had not had a particular creed and belief, they would have been like other rebels of the periods after them, but they did have a belief and later on this very belief found some kind of independent existence. Although they never managed to form a government, they did manage to create a school of law and a literature of their own.

There were individuals who never got around to actual rebellion, although they believed in it, as it is said of 'Amr ibn 'Ubayd and other Mu'tazilah. It was said of some of the Mu'tazilah who had beliefs similar to the *khawārij* about "bidding to good and forbidding evil", or about the matter of those Muslims who are guilty of moral sin still finding a place in paradise, that "they thought like the *khawārij*".

Thus there is a degree of commonality between the lexical meaning of the word and its particular reference.

thing that ʻAlī had done before but which had not been accepted. Even now they had not accepted it; it was a subterfuge for them to find a way to save themselves and rescue themselves from a sure defeat.

ʻAlī cried out: "Strike at them! They are using the pages and the paper of the Qur'ān as a ruse, they want to protect themselves behind the words and writing of the Qur'ān and afterwards carry on in their same old anti-Qur'ānic way. When opposed to its truth, the paper and binding of the Qur'ān is of no value and worthy of no respect; it is I who am the reality and the true manifestation of the Qur'ān. They are using the paper and the writing of the Qur'ān as an excuse to destroy its truth and meaning!"

A group of undiscriminating, unknowing and sanctimonious persons, who formed a sizeable proportion, gesticulate to each other. What does ʻAlī mean? They called out: "Should we fight against the Qur'ān? Our battle is to reestablish the Qur'ān, and now they have submitted to the Qur'ān, so what are we fighting for?"

"I also say I am fighting for the Qur'ān," said ʻAlī. "But they have no connection with the Qur'ān. They have put up the words and writing of the Qur'ān as a means to save their own souls."

There is a question in Islamic law, in the section on *jihād*, concerning the situation of unbelievers shielding themselves behind Muslims. The problem is that if the enemies of Islam put a group of Muslim prisoners of war at the front of their ranks as a shield, and they themselves are busy with their activities, making headway behind this front, so that if the Islamic forces try to defend themselves, or attack them and halt their advance, there is no alternative but to also eliminate, through necessity, their Muslims brothers who have become a shield; that is, if there is no possibility of access to the combatting and attacking enemy apart from through the killing of Muslims, then in this situation the killing of a Muslim for the vital interests of Islam, and so as to save the lives of the rest of the Muslims, becomes permissible in Islamic law.. In fact, they too are soldiers of Islam and will have become martyrs in the way of God. However, blood money must be paid for them from the Islamic treasury to their surviving relatives. This is, of course, not only a particuliarity of Islamic law, but there is a quite definite law among the international rules and regulations of war and military action that if the enemy wishes to use your own forces, you can eliminate those forces so as to reach the enemy and force them back.[5]

"If, when there are real, live Muslims," continued 'Alī, "and Islam says 'Attack!' so as to ensure a Muslim victory, then there can be no objection made to the paper and bindings of books. Respect for pages and writing is because of their meaning and contents. Today the fighting is for the contents of the Qur'ān, but these people have set up the pages as a means for the destruction of the meaning and contents of the Qur'ān."

However, the ignorant and uninformed drew down a black curtain in front of their minds and kept out the truth. "In addition to the fact that we will not fight with the Qur'ān," they said, "we know that fighting with it is itself a sin, and we must kill so as prevent this. We will fight with those who fight against the Qur'ān." Only an hour was needed to secure a victory; Mālik al-Ashtar, who was a brave, devoted and unselfish officer, had thus gone out to destroy the pavillion of Mu'āwiyah's command and to clear the path of Islam of obstacles. At this very moment, this group pressured 'Alī by saying they would attack from behind. 'Alī urged them not to, but they increased their protest, and, what is more, showed that they would be completely obstinate.

'Alī sent a message to Mālik to stop the fighting and to return from the place where the fighting was. He sent an answer back to 'Alī that if he were to give his permission for a few moments more the battle would be

5. For further reference, the section on *jihād* in the French translation of *Sharā'i'u 'l-Islam* by al-Muḥaqīq al-Ḥillī (Arabic text, 4 vols., Najaf 1389/1969) may be consulted. See *Droit Musulman, Recueil des lois concernant les Musulmans Schyites* translation by A. Querry (Paris 1871).

finished, and the enemy destroyed. But the Khawārij drew their swords and threatened to hack ʿAlī to pieces unless he called him back.

Then again word was sent to him that if he wanted to see ʿAlī alive, he should stop the battle and come back. He returned, and the enemy were jubilant that their stratagem had proved efficacious.

The fighting stopped so that they could leave arbitration to the Qur'ān. An arbitration committee was set up, and arbitrators selected from the two sides to rule on the basis of what was agreed on by both sides in the Qur'ān and *sunnah* and to bring an end to hostilities; or else they would add another difference to the already existing differences and cause the situation to deteriorate.

ʿAlī said that they should choose their arbitrator, and then he would detail his own. Without the slightest dispute, they unanimously chose ʿAmr ibn al-ʿĀṣ, the deviser of the stratagem. ʿAlī proposed ʿAbdullāh ibn al-ʿAbbās, who was versed in potitics, or Mālik al-Ashtar, a self-sacrificing, clearsighted man of faith, or else someone like them. But those fools were looking for someone of their own kind, and they chose a man of the like of Abū Mūsā al-Ashʿarī, a man of no perspicacity who was not on good terms with ʿAlī. However much ʿAlī and his friends sought to enlighten these people that Abū Mūsā was not the man for the job and that such an appointment was not suitable for him, they said that they would not agree to anyone else. Then he said that since things had got to that point, they should do whatever they wanted. So, in the end, they chose this Abū Mūsā as the arbitrator from the side of ʿAlī and his companions.

After months of consultation, ʿAmr ibn al-ʿĀṣ said to Abū Mūsā that it would be better for the interests of the Muslims if neither ʿAlī nor Muʿāwiyah were caliph, that they should choose a third one, and that there was no one else they could choose but ʿAbdullāh ibn ʿUmar, Abū Mūsā's son-in-law. Abū Mūsā said that that was right and asked what they should do. ‘Amr ibn al-‘Āṣ said: “You should remove ‘Alī from the caliphate, and I will do the same with Mu‘āwiyah. Then the Muslims will go and elect a worthy person who will surely be ‘Abdullāh ibn ‘Umar. Thus the roots of sedition will be destroyed.”

They terminated on this matter and announced that the people should gather together to listen to their conclusions.

The people assembled. Abū Mūsā turned towards ‘Amr ibn al-‘Āṣ to stand up and announce his opinion. ‘Amr ibn al-‘Āṣ said: “Me? You are the respected, white-bearded man, a companion of the Prophet. Never would I presume such a thing as to speak before you!”

Abū Mūsā moved from his place to rise and speak. Now everyone’s heart was beating fast, all eyes were staring, each person held his breath, waiting to see what the result had been. He started to speak: “After due deliberation on what was in the interests of the community, we saw that neither ‘Alī nor Mu‘āwiyah should be caliph. More than this it is not for us to say, for the Muslims themselves know what they wish.” The he took his ring from the finger of his right hand and said: “I have removed ‘Alī from the caliphate, just as I remove this ring from my finger.”

When he had finished he stepped down. Then ‘Amr ibn al-‘Āṣ got up and said: ‘You have all heard the speech of Abū Mūsā saying that he has removed ‘Alī from the caliphate. I too remove him from the caliphate, just as Abū Mūsā has done.” Then he took his ring off his right hand and then put it onto his left hand, and said: “I set up Mu‘āwiyah in the caliphate, just as I put this ring on my finger.” When he had said this he stepped down.

The meeting lapsed into commotion. The people began to attack Abū Mūsā, and some beat him with their whips. He fled to Mecca, and ‘Amr ibn al-‘Āṣ went to Damascus.

The Khawārij, who had brought about this sequence of events, saw the scandal of this arbitration with their own eyes, and realised their mistake. But they could not understand where exactly their error lay. They did not say that their mistake lay in falling for Mu'āwiyah and 'Amr ibn al-'Āṣ' scheme and bringing the war to a halt; nor did they say that after the setting up of the arbitration they had blundered in choosing their "referee", in putting up Abū Mūsā as 'Amr ibn al-'Āṣ' counterpart. No; instead they said that in putting up two human beings to arbitrate and be "referees" in the matters of the religion of God they had gone against the divine law and had done an act of unbelief, for the judge is only God, not man.

They came to 'Alī and said: "We did not understand. We chose a man as an arbitrator. You have become an unbeliver, and so have we. But we repent; you too should repent. Otherwise, the tragedy will be repeated."

"In any situation," said 'Alī, "repentance is good. We are always repenting for our sins." But they said this was not enough, and that he had to confess that arbitration was a sin, and that he repented of that sin. But he said that it had not been he that had brought about the affair of arbitration, it had been them, and that they had seen the result themselves. What was more, how could he declare as a sin something that Islam had made lawful, or confess to a sin which he had not perpetrated.

From this point on, they set to work as a religious sect. At the beginning they were a rebellious and mutinous group, and it was for that reason that they were called "Khawārij", but they gradually drew up basic beliefs for themselves and created a "party" that only had a political colouring to begin with but which step by step assumed the form of a religious group, taking on a religious colouring. Afterwards the Khawārij moved into action as a vehemently propagandist group as supporters of a religious sect. They eventually got the idea that they had discovered a worldly, corrupt root in Islam, and they came to the conclusion that 'Uthmān, 'Alī and Mu'āwiyah were all in error and sin. They decided that they had to struggle against this corruption that had come into existence, and they gave it the name of "bidding to good and forbidding evil." Thus the Khawārij sect came into existence under this banner.

Now, "bidding to good and forbidding evil" has, before anything else, two fundamental principles: one is a profound and knowledgeable insight into the religion, and the other is a profound insight into how to act. If there is no profound knowledge of religion, as we learn from *aḥādīth* (traditions), the loss that will be incurred in doing this will be greater than its benefit. And a profound insight into the correct way to act depends on two conditions which are called, in Islamic jurisprudence, *iḥtimālu 't-ta'thīr*, that is, the possibility of effective action, and *'adamu tarattub-i 'l-mafsadatin 'alayh*, that is, the absence of any resulting cause of evil, and this can only come about by the exercising of reason in these two duties.[6]

6. What we mean here is that *amr bi 'l-ma'rūf wa nahy 'ani 'l-munkar* (bidding to good and forbidding evil) has as its purpose that *ma'rūf* (that which is good, beneficial) should be propagated and *munkar* (that which is detestable, atrocious) be effaced. Thus there must be bidding to good and forbidding of evil in a place where there is the possibility of the desired effect coming about. If we know that there will definitely be no effect, how can it continue to be an obligation?

Moreover, the purpose in the legal (in Islamic terms) basis of this activity is that what is of advantage should be carried out. Thus it must obviously take place in a situation where there will not result any greater disadvantage. The requisite for these two conditions, then, is a thorough understanding of how to act correctly. A man who is lacking in this knowledge cannot foresee whether the desired result of this action will follow or not, or whether some greater evil will be produced or not. This is why the corruption resulting from ignorant inciting to good will be greater than its benefit, just as has been related in *ḥadīth*.

In the context of other duties, it has not been laid down as a condition that there must exist the possibility of their producing a useful result, and that if there is that possibility they become obligatory, otherwise not. Although something useful and of benefit manifests itself in every duty, the recognition of that benefit is not the responsibility of people. It has not been said about prayer, for example, that if you ⇒

The Khawārij had neither a profound knowledge of religion, nor a profound insight into prudent action; they were people of ignorance, lacking in any profound knowledge. In fact, they rejected any kind of profound knowledge of how to act, because they understood this duty to be a matter of obedience and they claimed that it should be performed blindly.

* * * * *

THE BASIS OF THE OPINIONS OF THE KHAWĀRIJ

The underlying root of Khawārijism is formed from the following four things:

a. They regarded 'Alī, 'Uthmān, Mu'āwiyah, the fighters at the battle of Jamal and those who accepted arbitration all as infidels, except those who voted for arbitration but afterwards repented.

⇐ see that it is useful then pray, and if you do not, then do not pray. Neither is it said about fasting that if it contains the possibility of producing something beneficial then fast, and if it does not have that posssibility then do not fast (only in fasting it is said that if you see there is harm in it, then do not fast), and likewise in *ḥajj* or *zakāt* or *jihād* there is no such restriction. But such a restriction does exist in the matter of bidding to good and forbidding evil, that one must look to see what kind of result, and what kind of reaction will be produced, and whether the action is in the interests of Islam and Muslims or not. That means that the discernment of the benefit is the responsibility of the very people who carry out this duty.

Everyone has a share in this duty, but it is necessary that he introduces reason, intelligence, knowledge of how to act correctly and attention to its benefit, and these latter things are not merely a matter of religious obligation.

This condition, that it is necessary to exercise a knowledge of effective action in bidding to good and forbidding evil, is unanimously agreed upon by all the sects of Islam except the Khawārij. Because of their particular inflexibility, rigidity and fanaticism, they said that bidding to good and forbidding evil is an absolute religious obligation; it has no condition of the possibility of a useful result or the absence of any corrupting influence; one must not sit down and think about it. It was in accordance with this belief that they rose up and terrorised the lands knowing that they would be killed and their blood would be wasted, and knowing that no useful result would come out of their uprising.

b. They regarded as infidels those who did not believe in the heresy of 'Alī, 'Uthmān and the others mentioned in (a).

c. Faith was not for them only sincere belief, but putting the commands into action and desisting from the prohibitions was also part of faith. Faith was a compound thing made up of belief and action.

d. There was an unconditional necessity to revolt against an unjust governor or leader. They believed that "bidding to good" and "forbidding evil" are not conditional on anything, and that in all circumstances this divine command must be carried out.

According to these opinions, these people started their existence from the recognition that all men on earth were infidels, whose blood was of no value and who were all condemned to the Fire.

* * * * *

WHAT THEY BELIEVED ABOUT THE CALIPHATE

The only idea of the Khawārij's that could be interpreted favourably by the modern thinkers of today is their theory about the caliphate. They had a quasi-democratic concept of it, and said that the caliph must be chosen by free election, and that the worthiest person was he who had merit as far as faith and piety were concerned. He could be from the Quraysh or not, from a distinguished and famous tribe, or from an insignificant and backward one, Arab or non-Arab.

If, after his election and after everyone had sworn allegiance to him, he took steps in a direction against the interests of the community of Islam, he should be removed from the caliphate, and if he refused, he should be fought with until killed.

In the matter of the caliphate they took a position opposite to that of the Shīʿah, who say that it is a divine office and that the caliph can only be someone who is nominated by God. They were also in opposition to the Sunnī, who say the caliphate belongs to the Quraysh and who hold firmly to the principle *innamā 'l-a'immatu min qurayshin* - "but the leaders are from the Quraysh."

Apparently their opinion about the caliphate was not something they had arrived at when they first came into existence. For, according to what their famous slogan *lā ḥukma illā li'llāh* - "no authority except Allāh's" - tells us, and also according to what we glean from *Nahju 'l-balāghah*,[7] they believed, in the beginning, that the people and the society did not need a leader or a government, and that the people should put the Book of God into practice on their own.

However, afterwards, they turned back on this belief and firmly swore allegiance to ʿAbdullāh ibn al-Wahab.[8]

* * * * *

WHAT THEY BELIEVED ABOUT THE CALIPHS

They recognised the caliphates of Abū Bakr and ʿUmar to be rightful, because they believed that these two persons had been rightfully elected and that they had not deviated from the way of the best interest, nor perpetrated anything against this best interest. They also recognised the election of ʿUthmān and ʿAlī to be rightful; however they said that towards the end of the sixth year of his caliphate, ʿUthmān changed his direction and ignored the best interest of the Muslims. So he should have been deposed from the caliphate, but since he continued in office he was killed as an unbeliever and his killing was a religious duty. As for ʿAlī, since he accepted the arbitration, but did not subsequently repent, he was killed as an unbeliever and his killing was a religious duty. Thus they

7. See sermon no. 40, and also the commentary of Ibn Abi 'l-Ḥadīd, vol. 2, p. 308.
8. See Ibn Kathīr, *al-Kāmil fī 't-tārīkh.*

denounced the caliphate of 'Uthmān after its seventh year, and that of 'Alī after the arbitration.[9]

They also abhorred the rest of the caliphs, and were always at war with them.

* * * * *

THE DECLINE OF THE KHAWĀRIJ

This group came into existence towards the end of the fourth decade of the first century of the Hijrah as the result of a dangerous piece of misrepresentation, and before one and half centuries were over, as the result of hysterical temerity and recklessness, they became the object of pursuance by the caliphs, which ended up with their own, and their sect's, annihilation and extermination, and at the beginning of the 'Abbāsid rule they had become totally non-existent. It was their relentless and spiritless logic, the severity and harshness of their behaviour, the incompatibility of their ways with real life, and, ultimately, their impetuosity (which even did away *taqīyah* [dissimulation][10] in its true and reasonable sense) which caused their ruin and destruction. The Khawārij sect was not one which could in any real sense survive, but its after-effect has remained; the thinking and beliefs of Khawārij have had an effect on the rest of the sects of Islam. Even today, "Nahrawānīs" are to be found in abundance, and, just as in the age and time of 'Alī, these are the most dangerous of Islam's internal enemies. Just as there always have been and always will be Mu'āwiyahs and 'Amr ibn al-'Āṣ's, who will use the existence of the "Nahrawānīs" when the time is opportune, even if they are counted as their enemies.

* * * * *

9. See ash-Shahrastānī, *al-Milal wa 'n-nihal*, Cairo, 1961.
10. On this doctrine, see 'Allāmah S. M. H. Ṭabā'ṭabā'ī : *Shī'ite Islam* (transl. S. H. Nasr) pp. 223-225. (tr.)

JUST A MOTTO?

To turn the discussion of Khawārijism and the Khawārij into a discussion about a religions sect is pointless and to no effect, for there is no such religious sect in existence in the world today. However, a discussion about the Khawārij and the reality of what they did is nevertheless instructive for us and for our society, because, although the Khawārij sect has become extinct, their spirit has not died. The spirit of Khawārijism has been incarnated in the campaigns of many of us.

I should start with an introduction. It is possible that some sects may die as far as their motto is concerned, but live in spirit, just as the opposite may also happen: an ideology may live as a motto but be completely dead in spirit. Thus it is possible that one or several individuals may be counted as followers and adherents of some sect in name but not be followers of that sect in spirit, and *vice versa*, that is, some people may follow some sect in spirit although they do not accept the motto and slogans of that sect.

To give an example well-known to all, right at the beginning, after the death of the Prophet, the Muslims divided up into two groups, Sunnī and Shī'ah; the Sunnī believe in one motto and one frame-work of beliefs, and the Shī'ah in another.

The Shī'ah say that the caliph immediately after the Prophet is 'Alī, and that he designated 'Alī for the caliphate and as his successor by divine decree. This position is thus 'Alī's by special right after the Prophet. But the Sunnī say that as far as the legislation of Islam is concerned, it has no special provisions in the matter of the caliphate or the Imāmate, rather the matter of choosing a leader was handed over to the people themselves. The most that can be said is that the choice should be made from among the Quraysh.

The Shī'ah have some criticisms to make of many of the Prophet's companions who are counted as great personalities, distinguished and famous men, while the Sunnī take a position complete opposed to that of the Shī'ah in this matter; they regard every person who was called a "companion" with an amazingly extravagant deference. They say that all the companions of the Prophet were just and upright men. The *raison d'être* of Shī'ite Islam is to work through criticism, research, putting forth objections and exactitude;[11] the *raison d'être* of Sunnī Islam to work through finding the most convenient solution, justification after the act and trust in providence.[12]

In the day and age in which we live, is it enough for us to recognise a man as a Shī'ah that he says: - "'Alī is the caliph immediately after the Prophet", without requiring anything more from him? No matter what spirit or what kind of way of thinking he may have?

However, if we were to return to the advent of Islam, we would meet with a particular way of thinking which would be the way of thinking of Shī'ite Islam, and it would be only those who thought in that way who could unreservedly accept the successorship to the Prophet as belonging to 'Alī without being subject to any doubt or wavering. Opposed to this spirit and this way of thinking was another spirit and way of thinking which, by a kind of justification, explanation or interpretation, ignored the successorships to the Prophet while having complete faith in him.

In fact, this Islamic "schism" sprung from here, for one group, who were, of course, the majority, only looked at the superficial aspect, not being sufficiently sharp-sighted or penetrating to reach the depth and truth of every reality. They saw what was most apparent and found the most convenient solution. They said that some of the great men, the

11. The original reads: "looking for a hair in their yogurt." (tr.)
12. The text reads, literally, "*inshā'allāh* it was a cat". This is a reference to a well-known story of a pious and learned *mullā* whose cloak was touched by a dog, thus rendering it impure (or, according to some versions, he was told after he had drunk from his bowl that it had been touched by a dog - the result is the same), and who thereupon said: "*inshā'allāh* it was a cat." The point is that the cat is not considered as a defiling animal. (tr.)

companions and elders, those who had served Islam for a long time, took a certain way, and it cannot be said that they were in error. But another group, who were the minority, said at the same time that they would respect anyone who respected the truth; however, where they saw that the fundamentals of Islam were violated at the hands of these very people who had served Islam for a long time, they would no longer respect them. They said they were partisans of the principles of Islam, not partisans of the personalities of Islam. Shīʿism came into existence in this spirit.

When, in the history of Islam, we follow in the tracks of Salmān al-Fārisī, Abū Dharr al-Ghifārī, al-Miqdād al-Kindī, ʿAmmār ibn Yāsir and the such like, and look to see what had persuaded them to gather round ʿAlī and leave the majority, we find that they were men of principle, who knew the fundamentals - that they both knew the religion and practised it. They said that they were not going to give their seeing and understanding into the hands of others, so that when these people made mistakes they themselves would also make mistakes. In reality the spirit of these people was a spirit over which principles and truths held command, not individuals and personalities.

One of ʿAlī's companions was badly seized by doubt during the battle of Jamal. He looked round about himself, and saw on one side ʿAlī and great figures of Islam who were gathered round him striking away with their swords; and on the other side he saw the wife of the Prophet, ʿĀ'ishah, about whom the Qur'ān said: وَأَزْوَاجُهُ أُمَّهَاتُهُمْ - *And his wives are as their mothers.* Gathered round ʿĀ'ishah he saw Ṭalḥah, one of the forerunners in Islam, a man with a good past record, an expert fighter in the field of battle for Islam, a man who had done valuable services for Islam; and he saw az-Zubayr, too, a man with an even better past record than Ṭalḥah, who had even been among those who had gathered in ʿAlī's house on the day of Saqīfah.[13]

This poor man was in a state of great bewilderment. What was going on!

13. For information on these persons and events see: S. H. M. Jafri: *The Origins and Early Development of Shīʿa Islam.* (London 1979), especially chps. 2 & 4. (tr.)

Are ‘Alī, Ṭalḥah and az-Zubayr not among the forerunners of Islam, the most devoted men, the strongest forts of Islam? Now they are fighting face to face. Who is the nearer to the truth? What must be done in this conflict?

But take care: this man must not be blamed too much in his confusion. Perhaps if we found ourselves in the same situation as he had found himself, the personalities of Ṭalḥah and az-Zubayr would also dazzle our eyes.

Now that we see ‘Alī and ‘Ammār, Uways al-Qaranī and others face to face with ‘Ā’ishah and az-Zubayr and Ṭalḥah, we do not feel any hesitation, for we wee the second group as people with the look of criminals, that is, the effects of evil and treachery are evident on their faces; and when we look at the faces and their characters we guess that they are people of the Fire. But if we had lived in those times, and had know their pasts from close-up, perhaps we would not have been immune from doubt.

Today, when we know that the first group were for truth and the second group for falsehood, it is because we have come to know ‘Alī and ‘Ammār, on the one hand, and az-Zubayr, Ṭalḥah and ‘Ā’ishah, on the other, as a result of history's passing and the clarification of the facts, and in this context we have been able to judge correctly. Or, at any rate, if we are not researchers and students of history, we have been inculcated with the idea that things were like this, right from our infancy. But in those days, neither of these factors existed.

Anyway, this man was able to come up to Amīr al-mu'minīn and say: "Is it possible that Ṭalḥah and az-Zubayr and ‘Ā’ishah are gathered together for falsehood? How can personalities like these great companions of the Messenger of God err, and follow the way of falsehood? Is such a thing possible?"
In his reply, ‘Alī said something about which Ṭāhā Ḥusayn, the Egyptian

scholar and writer has said that no more forceful or greater thing has been said. He wrote that after the revelation had ceased and the call from heaven had come to an end, words with such greatness as these were not heard.[14] 'Alī said:

> "It is you who have been cheated; truth has become an error for you. Truth and falsehood are not to be known by the measure of the power and personality of individuals. It is not right that you should first measure up the personalities, and then weigh truth and falsehood according to these weights: this is true because it accords with this, and that is false because it does not accord with this. No, individuals must not be made the criteria for truth and falsehood. It is truth and falsehood which should be the standards for individuals and their personalities."

This means that one should be a knower of truth and falsehood, not a knower of individuals and personalities; one should measure individuals, whether they be great personalities or small, according to truth - if they accord with it, then accept their personalities, if not, then leave them. Then there is no question as to whether Ṭalḥah, az-Zubayr and 'Ā'ishah are with falsehood or not.

Here 'Alī establishes truth itself as the criterion of truth, and the spirit of Shī'ite Islam is none other than this. In fact, the Shī'ah sect is born from a special perspicacity and a granting of importance to principles, not from individuals and persons. It is natural that the Shī'ah were the first believers and idol-breakers.

After the death of the Prophet, 'Alī was thirty-three years old with a small group less than the number of the fingers on one's hands; opposing him - were old men of sixty years with a large and numerous majority. The logic of the majority was that this was the way of the leaders and the Shaykhs, and they do not make mistakes, so their way must be followed. The logic of the minority was that that which does not err is the truth,

14. In *'Alī wa banūh* ('Alī and His Sons), p. 40.

the elders must accord themselves - with the truth. And for this reason it can be understood how numerous are the people whose motto is the motto of Shī'ite Islam, but whose spirit is not the spirit of Shī'ite Islam.

The way of Shī'ism is just like its spirit: the discernment of truth and the pursuance of it. And one of the greatest effects of this is attraction and repulsion. Not any attraction or any repulsion - we have said that attraction is sometimes attraction to falsehood, evil and crime, and repulsion is sometimes repulsion from the truth and human virtues - but attraction and repulsion of the like of attraction and repulsion to 'Alī. Because the true Shī'ah is a copy of 'Alī's conduct; the Shī'ah must also, like 'Alī, have two sides to his character.

This introduction was so that we should know that a religious sect may be dead, but its spirit lives on among other people who apparently are not followers of that sect but who deem themselves opposed to it. The Khawārij sect is dead, that is to say that today, on this earth, there is no observable group with the name of Khawārij which a number of persons, with that name, follow; but is the spirit of the Khawārij dead too? Has this spirit not incarnated itself, for example (may God forbid it), among us, especially among those of us who are, so to speak, pretenders to piety?

This is a matter which must be investigated separately. If we can truly recognise the Khawārij spirit, we can perhaps answer this question. This is, indeed, the value of a discussion about the Khawārij. We must know why 'Alī "repelled" them, that is to say, why his attraction did not pull them, but, on the contrary, his power of repulsion pushed them away.

It is certain, as we shall afterwards see, that not all the spiritual elements which had an effect on the personality of the Khawārij and the formation of their way of thinking were such as to be subject to the pressure and rule of 'Alī's force of repulsion. A good many bright distinctions and positive points are also to be found in their way of thinking, which, if they had not been there together with a series of dark points, would have been subject to the power and effect of 'Alī's power of attraction. But the dark side of their spirit was so strong that they took their place in the ranks of 'Alī's enemies.

* * * * *

'ALĪ'S SENSE OF DEMOCRACY

'Alī acted towards the Khawārij with the utmost degree of liberality and democracy. He was the caliph and they were his subjects; every kind of punitive action was within his power, but he did not put them into prison, neither did he flog them; he did not even cut off their quota from the treasury (*baytu 'l-māl*). He looked upon them in the same way as upon other individuals. This matter is no exception in the history of 'Alī's life, but it is something of which there are few examples in the world. Everywhere they were free to express their opinions, and 'Alī and his companions freely opposed them with their own opinions and spoke to them. The two sides put forth their reasoning, and countered their opponent's reasoning.

Maybe such a degree of freedom is without precedent in the world, in which a government acts towards its opponents with such a degree of democracy. They came into the mosques and disrupted 'Alī's speeches and sermons. One day, 'Alī was speaking from the minbar when a man came forward and asked a question, and 'Alī gave an impromptu answer. A Khawārij who was among the people called out: "May God kill this man; what a knowledgeable man he is!" The others wanted to hold him back, but 'Alī ordered them to release him, saying: "It was only me he insulted."

The Khawārij would not pray behind 'Alī in communal prayers because they considered him a disbeliever, but they went to the mosque and refused to let 'Alī alone, sometimes molesting him. One day, 'Alī had stood up to pray and the people had stoop up behind him, when one of the Khawārij whose name was Ibn al-Kawwā' shouted out, and read a verse from the Qur'ān in allusion to 'Alī

This verse was addressed to the Prophet:

وَلَقَدْ أُوحِيَ إِلَيْكَ وَإِلَى الَّذِينَ مِن قَبْلِكَ لَئِنْ أَشْرَكْتَ لَيَحْبَطَنَّ عَمَلُكَ وَلَتَكُونَنَّ مِنَ الْخَاسِرِينَ

And indeed it has been revealed to thee and to those (prophets) before thee, "If thou associatest (other gods with Allāh), thy work shall surely fail and thou wilt be among the losers." (az-Zumar, 39:65)

Ibn al-Kawwā' wanted to insinuate about 'Alī by reciting this verse that: "Yes, we know your past history in Islam! First you were a believer, the Prophet chose you as a brother, your selflessness shone out on the night of the Prophet's escape from Mecca (*laylatu 'l-mabīt*) when you slept in the place of the Prophet in his bed, you put yourself forward as a lure for swords. Truly your service for Islam cannot be denied. But God also said to His Prophet: 'If you associate (others with God) your work will come to naught.' Now that you have become a disbeliever you have cancelled out your past deeds."

What could 'Alī do, faced with this, with this man's voice shouting out the Qur'ān? He remained silent until the man reached the end of the verse; and when he finished, 'Alī continued with the prayer. Then Ibn al-Kawwā' repeated the verse, and meanwhile 'Alī fell silent again. He kept silent because it is a Qur'ānic command that:

وَإِذَا قُرِئَ الْقُرْآنُ فَاسْتَمِعُوا لَهُ وَأَنصِتُوا

And when the Qur'ān is recited, give you ear to it and be silent. (al-A'rāf, 7:204)

And this is the proof for the fact that when the prayer-leader is reciting the Qur'ān, believers must be silent and listen.

After he had repeated the verse several times, wanting to disrupt the prayer, 'Alī recited this verse:

فَاصْبِرْ إِنَّ وَعْدَ اللهِ حَقٌّ ۖ وَلَا يَسْتَخِفَّنَّكَ الَّذِينَ لَا يُوقِنُونَ

> *So be thou patient: surely Allāh's promise is true; and let not those who have not sure faith make thee unsteady.* (ar-Rūm, 30:60)

Then he paid no more attention and continued with his prayer.[15]

* * * * *

THE RISING-UP AND INSURRECTION OF THE KHAWĀRIJ

In the beginning, the Khawārij were peaceable, and contented themselves with merely criticising and speaking openly. 'Alī's behaviour with them was also just as we noted before, namely, he never caused them any trouble, not even cutting off their wages from the treasury (*baytu 'l-māl*). However, as they began to despair of 'Alī ever repenting, their activities gradually changed. They decided to bring about a revolution, so they gathered in the house of one of their brethren, who gave an aggressive and provocative speech in which he invited his friends to rise up in the name of "bidding to good and forbidding evil." He said (after praise to God):

> I swear by God that it is not worthy of a group which has faith in a Merciful God and which adheres to the command of the Qur'ān that the world should seem dearer to them than "bidding to good and forbidding evil" and speaking the truth, even though these (activities) may bring loss and involve danger; for everyone who incurs loss and danger in this world will be rewarded on the Day of the Resurrection with the felicity of God and the eternity of Paradise. O brothers! Le us go out from this city where injustice dwells (and go) to mountainous places or some other towns so that

15. *Sharḥ*, Ibn Abi 'l-Ḥadīd, vol. 6, p. 311.

we can take a stand against these misguided innovations and put a stop to them.

With this morale-raising and fiery speech, they became even more fiery and went out from that place to try to bring about an uprising and a revolution. They threatened the security of the highways and took to marauding and sedition. Their aim was to weaken the government by this means, and to bring down the then existent rule.

Now it was no longer the time to leave them at liberty, for it was not a matter of the expression of beliefs. but of sabotage against pulic security and an armed uprising against the legal government. Thus ʿAlī pursued them and met them face to face on the banks of the Nahrawān. He made a speech in which he advised them and gave them an incontrovertible proof. Then he put the flag of true faith into the hands of Abū Ayyūb al-Anṣāri as a sign that everyone who gathered round it was a true believer. Out of twelve thousand men, eight thousand turned back from Khawārijism while the remainder showed their obstinacy. They were severely beaten, and apart from a very small band none remained.

* * * * *

THE DISTINGUISHING FEATURES OF THE KHAWĀRIJ

The spirit of the Khawārij is a very special one. They were a mixture of the ugly and the beautiful, and, as a whole, were such as to take their place in the end among the enemies of ʿAlī. ʿAlī's personality "repulsed" them, it did not "attract" them.

We shall mention both the positive and beautiful aspects and the negative and ugly aspects of their spirit which, when combined, made them dangerous and even horrifying.

1. They had the spirit of struggle and self-sacrfce, and they strived valiantly in the way of their beliefs and ideas. In the history of the Khawārij, we find completely altruistic men who have few equals in the history of mankind, and their altruism and self-sacrifice was the life of their bravery and their power.

Ibn ʻAbdu Rabbih said about them: "Among all the sects, none were more convinced or exerted more effort than the Khawārij, and also none could be found more ready to die than them. One of them was once hit by a spear and the spear had gone deep into him. Even then, he rushed towards his killer saying: 'O God! I am hurrying towards you so that you may be pleased'."

Muʻāwiyah sent a man after his son who was a Khawārij so as to bring him back, but the father was unable to make his son change his mind. In the end, he said: "My son, I will go and bring your infant child that the sight of him together with your fatherly instincts may bring you to your senses and force you to give this up." The son replied: "I swear by God, I am more eager for sword-thrusts than for my son!"

2. They were people of worship and devotion, they spent their nights in prayer and were without any desire for the world and its charms. When ʻAlī sent Ibn ʻAbbās to admonish the people of the battle of Nahrawān, he came back and described them as twelve thousand men whose foreheads had been calloused by an excess of prostration, whose hands had become hard like camels' feet from being so frequently pressed to the dry, burning ground and from striking the dust before their Lord, whose shirts were tattered and worn down to their skins, but who were unwavering and determined.

The Khawārij were strictly obedient to the laws and outward practices of Islam; they never put their hands to anything they considered a sin. They had their own principles and standards, and they never mixed these with principles against their own; they showed their disgust with anyone who was tainted with sin. Ziyād ibn Abīh killed one of them and then sent for the man's slave and enquired of him what kind of a man he had been. The slave said that he had never brought food for him during the day, nor laid out his bedding at night; during the day he had fasted and he had spent the nights in prayer.

Wherever they placed their footsteps, they referred back to their beliefs and they were devout in all their actions. They would kill to forward their beliefs.

'Alī (a.s.) said of them:

> Do not kill any Khawārij after me, because one who seeks the truth and errs is not the same as one who seeks falsehood and finds it.[16]

He meant that they were different from those around Mu'āwiyah, for they wanted truth, but had fallen into error, whereas those around Mu'āwiyah were imposters from the start whose way was that of falsehood. Thus if they were to kill the Khawārij after 'Alī had gone it would be to the advantage of Mu'āwiyah who was worse and more dangerous than them.

It is necessary, before we go on to describe the other particuliarities of the Khawārij, to remember one point, since we are talking about their pretension to devotion, piety and asceticism. One of the wonderful, distinctive and extraordinary points in the history of the life of 'Alī, whose like cannot be found, is his courageous and brave stand when fighting against these fossilised and haughty pietists.

In front of people who clung to, and adorned themselves with, the externals of devotion, and whose faces affected truth, whose clothes were in tatters and who were professional worshippers, 'Alī drew his sword and subjected them all to its sharp edge.

Surely, if we had been in the place of his companions and had seen the

16. *Nahju 'l-balāghah*, Sermon no. 60.

face of these people, our feelings would have been moved, and we would have remonstrated with ʿAlī about drawing swords against such people.

This story of the Khawārij is one of the most edifying lessons for the history of Shīʿism in particular, and for the world of Islam in general.

ʿAlī was himself aware of the importance and the exceptional nature of what action he took in these circumstances, as he recounted when he said:

فَإِنِّي فَقَأْتُ عَيْنَ الْفِتْنَةِ، وَلَمْ يَكُنْ لِيَجْتَرِئَ عَلَيْهَا أَحَدٌ غَيْرِي بَعْدَ أَنْ مَاجَ غَيْهَبُهَا، وَاشْتَدَّ كَلَبُهَا

> *I have put out the eye of revolt. No-one had the daring to do this except me when its gloom had surged up and its rabidity had become severe.*[17]

Amīr al-mu'minīn (a.s.) gives two interesting expressions here. One is its "gloom", which causes doubt and uncertainty. The manner of the external saintliness and piety of the Khawārij was such that every believer with strong faith became again uncertain; and in this sense a dark and vague atmosphere was created, a space which became filled with doubt and hesitation.

The other is that he likened the condition of these pietists to rabies, that is to hydrophobia, the madness which exists in dogs so that they bite anyone they come across. Since such a dog is a carrier of an infectious microbial disease, when the fangs of the dog penetrate the body of any man or animal, and something enters the blood of the man or animal from its saliva, this man or animal after a short while becomes afflicted with this disease; he too becomes rabid and bites and makes others rabid. This is why wise people will immediately kill a rabid dog; so that at least they can save others from the danger of rabies.

---

17. *ibid.*, Sermon no. 92.

'Alī said that they behaved like rabid dogs; they were not curable; they bit and infected and regularly added to the number of cases of rabies.

Alas, for the condition of the Muslim community of that time. A pietistic, one-geared, ignorant and uninformed group were walking around on one foot and falling on this soul or that. What power could stand up against these charmed snakes? Where was the strong and powerful spirit that would not waver before these ascetic and pious faces? Where was the hand which would raise itself to bring down a sword on their heads without trembling? This is what 'Alī meant when he said that no-one had the daring to do this except he. Apart from 'Alī and his insight and firm faith, no-one of the Muslims, who believed in God, the Prophet and the Resurrection dared to unsheath their swords against them. Only someone who did not believe in God and Islam could have dared to kill this kind of people, not the ordinary believer.

It was this that 'Alī mentioned as a kind of great honour for himself: It was I, and only I, who realised the great danger that was pointing from the direction of these piestists towards Islam. Neither their calloused foreheads, nor the ascetic-like clothes, nor their forever God-remembering tongues, nor even their strong and steadfast beliefs, could become an obstacle to my insight into them. It was I who understood that if they got a footing everyone would be afflicted with their blight, that the world of Islam would become inflexible, adhering to the external aspects, superficial and fossilised, that Islam's back would become bent. Is it not this that the Prophet mentioned: Two groups will break my back - those who know but act recklessly, and those who are ignoranct but profess piety.

'Alī wanted to say that if he had not fought against the Khārijite movement in the Islamic world, no other person would have come forward and dared to fight against them. Apart from him there was no-one who saw that those whose foreheads were calloused by excessive prostrations were pious and religious men but a barrier in the way of

Islam, people who saw themselves as working to the advantage of Islam, but who were in fact the real enemies of Islam; there was no-one to fight against them and spill their blood. Only he could do that.

What 'Alī did smoothed the path for the subsequent caliphs and rulers so that they could fight against the Khawārij and kill them; so that the soldiers of Islam also would obey them without any why or wherefore; for 'Alī had fought with them. In fact, 'Alī's conduct also opened the way for others so that they could, without fear, fight against any group that showed itself to be outwardly pious, to have pretentions to saintliness and to be religious, but who were really fools.

3. The Khawārij were ignorant and unknowing people, and because of their ignorance and lack of knowledge they could not understand realities, and wrongly interpreted events. Gradually this warped understanding of things took the form of a religion or faith in the process of establishing which they exerted themselves to their greatest self-sacrifices. In the beginning, the Islamic precept of forbidding evil shaped them into the form of a party whose only aim was to revive an Islamic practice.

Here it is necessary to pause and reflect more carefully on a point from Islamic history. When we refer back to the life of the Prophet, we see that in the whole of the thirteen year Meccan period he never gave permission for *jihād* or even for defensive warfare to anyone, to the point that the Muslims really got into straits, and, with the Prophet's permission, a group emigrated to Abyssinia. However the rest remained and suffered persecution; it was only in the second year in Medina that permission was given for *jihād*. In the Meccan period the Muslims saw the teachings; they became acquainted with the spirit of Islam. The Islamic way of life penetrated into the depths of their spirits, with the result that after their entering Medina each one of them was a true emissary for Islam, and the Prophet of Islam, who sent them all over the region, was able to employ them to advantage. Also, when they were sent to do *jihād*, they knew what they were fighting for. In the words of Amīr al-mu'minīn (a.s.):

حَمَلُوا بَصَائِرَهُمْ عَلَى أَسْيَافِهِمْ

They linked their profound understanding with their swords.

Their swords were thus tempered and the men so well-instructed that they could accomplish their mission within the limits set by Islam. When we read history and see what these men said who, till a few years previously, had known nothing but the sword and the camel, we are overwhelmed and amazed by their lofty ideas and their profound practice of Islam.

In the time of the caliphs, most regretfully, more attention was directed towards conquests, ignoring the fact that, along with opening wide the gates of Islam towards others, and pointing them in the direction of Islam, when anyhow they were attracted by the monotheism of Islam and its justice and equality towards Arab and non-Arab, it was necessary to teach Islamic culture and its way of life and make people thoroughly aware of the spirit of Islam.

The Khawārij were mostly Arabs, although there were also several non-Arabs; but all of them, Arab or not, were ignorant of the principles, and unaquainted with the culture, of Islam. They wanted to redress all their shortcomings by empahsis on prostration. 'Alī (a.s.) described their morale in these words:

> People who are crude, lacking lofty ideas or subtle feelings; people who are feeble, like slaves, rogues assembled from every corner, come together from all quarters. They are people who should first of all be instructed, taught Islamic behaviour, and who should acquire skill in how to live as true Muslims. A guardian should rule over them and take them by the hand, they should not be left free, to keep swords in their hands, and to voice their opinions about Islam. They are neither emigrés (from Mecca) who have fled from their homes for Islam nor Anṣār (of Medina) who welcomed the emigrés among themselves.

The appearance of an ignorant stratum of the community with beliefs affecting false piety, of which the Khawārij were a part, was to Islam's great cost. Forgetting, for the moment, the Khawārij, who, with all their drawbacks, were endowed with the virtues of bravery and self-sacrifice, another group came into existence from this pietistic trend who did not have these virtues. These people pulled Islam towards monasticism and retreat from the world, they were responsible for the widespread occurrence of pretension and sanctimoniousness. Since they did not possess the above virtues with which they could wield the steel sword against those in power, they wielded the sword of words against those who possessed learning. They made it a custom to call the learned unbelievers, immoralists and irreligious.

At any rate, one of the most evident distinguishing features of the Khawārij was their ignorance and lack of knowledge, and one of the manifestations of their ignorance was their inability to distinguish between the outward nature of the Qur'ān, that is, its writing and binding, and its meaning, and thus it was that they fell for the trick of the easy ruse of Mu'āwiyah and 'Amr ibn al-'Āṣ.

With these people, ignorance and worship went hand in hand. 'Alī wanted to fight against their ignorance, but how could he separate the ascetic, pious and devotional side of them from their aspect of ignorance, since their devotion was the very same as their ignorance? For 'Alī, whose acquaintance with Islam was of the first degree, worship hand in hand with ignorance was of absolutely no value. Therefore he destroyed them, and they could not use their asceticism, piety and devotion as a shield between themselves and 'Alī.

The danger of the ignorance of this kind of people, and the more so of this kind of group, is the way in which they become tools and instruments in the hands of the cunning, and a barrier to the way which is in the higher interests of Islam. Irreligious hypocrites can always incite simple pietists against the interests of Islam; they become swords in these people's hands, and arrows in their bows.

'Alī explained this characteristic of theirs in a very sublime and subtle way, when he said:

ثُمَّ أَنْتُمْ شِرَارُ النَّاسِ، وَمَنْ رَمَى بِهِ الشَّيْطَانُ مَرَامِيَهُ، وَضَرَبَ بِهِ تِيهَهُ!

Thus you are the worst of people; you are arrows in the hand of Satan which he uses to strike his target, and through you he casts people into confusion and doubt.

We have said that in the beginning the Khārijite party came into existence to keep alive an Islamic tradition, but that lack of insight and unknowing dragged them to the point where they misinterpreted the verses of the Qur'ān. It was from here that they began to take on a religious colouring and become delineated as a sect and as a way. There is a verse in the Qur'ān which says:

إِنِ الْحُكْمُ إِلَّا لِلَّهِ ۖ يَقُصُّ الْحَقَّ ۖ وَهُوَ خَيْرُ الْفَاصِلِينَ

The judgement (ḥukm) is Allāh's alone, He relates the truth and He is the Best of deciders. (Al-An'am, 6:57)

In this verse, *ḥukm* has been explained as one of the special attributes of God's essence, but it is necessary to see what the meaning of *ḥukm* is.

Without doubt, the meaning of *ḥukm* (judgement) here is the law and order of man's life. In this *āyah*, the right to lay down the law has been denied to any other than God, and this has been recognised as one of the degrees of God's essence (or of a person who has been given authority by God). But the Khawārij took *ḥukm* in the meaning of *ḥukūmah* (government), which also contains the idea of *hakamīyah* (arbitration), and made their own slogan: *lā ḥukma illā li'llāh* - government and arbitration is Allāh's alone. Their intention was that government (*ḥukūmah*), arbitration (*hakamīyah*) and leadership too, just as law-giving, was the special right of God, and that, apart from God, no-one had the right to arbitrate among, or govern, people, just as they had no right to create laws.

Once Amīr al-mu'minīn was at prayer (or maybe addressing people from the minbar) when they called out and addressed him: *lā ḥukma illā li'llāh, lā laka wa li aṣḥābik* - O 'Alī, governing is only for God. It is not for you or your friends to govern or arbitrate!

In reply, he said:

> The sentence is right but what (they think) it means is wrong. It is true that law-giving (*ḥukm*, judgement) is God's alone, but these people say that governance is God's alone. The fact is that men need a governor, a ruler, whether he is good or (maybe) bad. Under (the shadow of) his rule, the believer performs good actions while the disbeliever profits from his worldly life; and God brings every thing to its end. Through the ruler, taxes are collected, enemies are fought, the roads are kept safe, and the rights of the weak are taken from the strong, so that the virtuous enjoy peace and are given protection from the wicked.[18]

In short, the law does not get put into practice all by itself; there must be someone, or some group, who tries to put it into practice.

4. They were narrow-minded and short-sighted people, whose thought evolved below very inferior horizons; they enclosed Islam and the Muslims within the four walls of their own limited ideas. Like all other narrow-minded people they claimed that everyone else had misunderstood, or had not understood at all; all had taken the wrong way and were destined for Hell. The first thing that this kind of narrow-minded person does is that he gives his narrow-mindedness the form of a religious belief; he restricts God's mercy, make Him sit forever on a throne of wrath, waiting for his slave to make some error so that He may cast him into eternal punishment. One of the fundamental beliefs of the Khawārij was that the perpetrator of any great sin, for example lying, backbiting or drinking alcohol, was a disbeliever (*kāfir*) and was beyond the pale of Islam, eternalled

18. *ibid.*, Sermon no. 40.

condemned to the Fire. Thus, apart from a very limited number of people, everyone was condemned to the Fire. Religious narrow-mindedness was a special characteristic of the Khawārij, but we see this once again among the Muslims today. It is for this reason that we said that the banner of the Khawārij is dead and gone but the spirit of their religion still lives on, to a greater or lesser extent, among similar individuals and groups.

We can find some bigots who look on all the people in the world except themselves and a very small number of people like themselves as disbelievers and infidels; they deem the number of those included within Islam and the Muslims to be very limited indeed.

We mentioned, in the previous chapter, that the Khawārij were not acquainted with the spirit of Islamic culture but that they were courageous. Since they were ignorant, they were narrow-minded; and since they were narrow-minded, they were quick to condemn people as infidels and iniquitous, to the point where they restricted the meaning of Islam and Muslim to themselves, and marked other Muslims who did not subscribe to their beliefs as infidels. Since they were courageous, they often came up to those in power and, according to what they imagined, subjected them to "bidding to good and forbidding evil", but then were killed themselves. We also said that in the subsequent periods of Islamic history their inflexibility, ignorance, pietism and pretensions to sanctity were inherited by others, but without their bravery, heroism and self-sacrifice. The non-heroic Khawārij, that is, the cowardly sactimonious ones, put their steel swords on one side, dispensing with "bidding to good and forbidding evil" as far as those in power were concerned, who were a danger to them, and then fell upon the learned with the sword of words. They brought some kind of accusation against every learned person so that few are the learned persons in Islamic history who have not been the target of the accusations of this group. They would call one a denier of God, another a denier of the Resurrection; a third they would call a denier of the bodily ascension of the Prophet (*mi'rāj-e jismānī*), a fourth a dervish, a fifth something else, and so forth. In this way, if the opinions of these half-wits were taken as a criterion, no real scholar could ever have been a Muslim. When 'Alī was charged with being an infidel, the position of others is clear. Ibn Sīnā, Naṣiru 'd-Dīn aṭ-Ṭūsī, Mullā Ṣadrā, Fayḍ al-Kāshānī, Sayyid Jamālu 'd-Dīn al-Asadābādī (al-Afghānī), and, more recently, Muḥammad Iqbāl are a few of those who have tasted the bitter draught of this cup. Ibn Sīnā wrote, in connection with this matter

Calling me an infidel is no easy exaggeration,
For there is no faith stronger than mine.
If at one time there is only one like me and he an infidel.
Was there ever a Muslim in any period?

Khwājah Naṣiru 'd-Dīn aṭ-Ṭūsī, who was accused of being an infidel by a person by the name of Niẓāmu 'l-'Ulamā' (the one who puts order among the learned) said:

If the "Organiser" who lacks order call me an infidel,
I can console myself that the lamp of falsity will never shine bright.
I shall call him a Muslim, for there is
No answer to a lie except a lie.

Anyway, one of the special characteristics of the Khawārij was narrow-mindedness, and it was their short-sightedness which called everyone irreligious. Against this short-sighted ness, 'Alī argued that it was a very mistaken way of thinking which they followed. He said that the Prophet would punish someone and then read the burial prayers over his corpse, whereas if the committing of a great sin made one an infidel, the Prophet would not have done this; for it is not permissible to recite prayers over the corpse of an unbeliever, being something which the Qur'ān has prohibited.[19] He gave lashes to the drinker of alcohol, cut off the hand of the thief, whipped the unmarried adulterer, and then gave them all a place in Muslim meetings, did not cut off their wages from

19. at-Tawbah, 9:84.

the treasury (*baytu 'l-māl*), and married them to other Muslims. The Prophet meted out Islam punishments as they were due, but he never crossed the names of the punished off the list of the Muslims. 'Alī asked the Khawārij to suppose that he had gone wrong, and that, as a result of that he had become an infidel. But why then did they condemn the Muslim community as infidels? Did that mean that because someone had gone astray the others too were necessarily lost and in error and should be called to account? He asked them why they carried their swords on their shoulders, and subjected the sinless and the sinners alike to the edge of their swords.[20]

Here Amīr al-mu'minīn objected to them on two accounts; his "repelling" repulsed them on two sides. One was that they had generalised the sin to those who were guiltless, and had taken them to account for it, and the other was that they deemed the perpetrator of sin as necessarily an infidel and outside of Islam, that is, they had restricted the extent of Islam and said that anyone who stepped beyond the limits of some of the prescriptions of Islam had stepped out of Islam.

'Alī condemned the narrow-minded and the short-sighted, and in reality the struggle of 'Alī with the Khawārij was a struggle with this way of thinking not a struggle with individuals. For, if these individuals had not thought in this way, 'Alī would not have behaved with them in the way he did and split their blood so that these ideas would die with them, that the Qur'ān would be correctly understood, and the Muslims would understand Islam and the Qur'ān as they are and as their Law-maker wished.

The result of this short-sightedness and crooked thinking was that they were taken in by the politics of holding the Qur'ān up on spears, and thereby created the greatest of dangers for Islam. And 'Alī, who had gone to dig out the root of hypocrisy and destroy Mu'āwiyah and his plotting once and for all, had to turn back and deal with them. What a

20. For the text of this sermon see *Nahju 'l-balāghah*, Sermon no. 126.

ominuous event it was which happened to the Muslim community on that occasion.[21]

21. In the assessment of most people, the most serious misfortunes that have befallen the world of Islam have been the spiritual blows which have fallen on the Muslims. The Qur'ān established the foundation of the call to Islam on true understanding and thinking, and itself recommends the way of striving after understanding (*ijtihād*) and intellective perception:

فَلَوْلَا نَفَرَ مِن كُلِّ فِرْقَةٍ مِّنْهُمْ طَائِفَةٌ لِّيَتَفَقَّهُوا فِي الدِّينِ

But why should not a party of every section of them go forth to acquire understanding (yatafaqahū) in religion? (at-Tawbah, 9:122)

"*tafaqqaha*" (to acquire understanding) is not used for easy understanding, but it is rather understanding through exercising effort and perspicacity.

إِن تَتَّقُوا اللَّهَ يَجْعَل لَّكُمْ فُرْقَانًا

if you fear Allāh, He will grant you a distinguishing (light). (al-Anfāl, 8:29)

وَالَّذِينَ جَاهَدُوا فِينَا لَنَهْدِيَنَّهُمْ سُبُلَنَا

But those who struggle in Our cause, surely We shall guide them in Our ways. (al-'Ankabūt, 29:69)

The Khawārij started an inflexibility and stagnation that was completely opposed to this way of teaching of the Qur'ān which wanted Islamic knowledge (*fiqh*) to remain for ever moving and alive. They conceived Islamic education as something deadening and motionless and dragged solid forms and shapes into Islam.

Islam has never been concerned just with forms, shapes and the outward manifestations of life; Islamic teachings are all directed to the spirit and meaning and the way in which man can reach that goal and these meanings. Islam has taken as part of its domain these goals and meanings and the guidance to the way to reach these goals, while it leaves man free in what is other than this, and thus it steers clear of any clash with the development of civilisation and true culture.

No material means or outward form can occur in Islam with a "sacred" side which Muslims could regard it their duty to preserve. And this avoidance of collision with the outward forms of scientific or cultural development is one reason why the conformity of the religion of Islam with the requirements of the times has been made easy, and any great obstacle to its continuing survival removed. ⇒

⇐ It is this very mixture of intellection and religiosity which has, on the one hand, been taken as the foundation, and which, on the other hand, divorces this latter from forms. It gives us universal considerations, and these universalities can take on a number of different outward manifestations without the changing of these manifestations causing any change in the truth.

However the harmonisation of the truth with its outward manifestations and referrents is not such an easy matter that anyone can do it, for it needs penetrating perception and genuine understanding. The Khawārij were people congealed in their thinking, distant from what they heard, and lacking the ability to understand. Thus when Amīr al-mu'minīn sent Ibn 'Abbās to argue with them, he said to him: "Do not reason with them by the Qur'ān, because the Qur'ān has many sides to it: you will speak and they will speak. But reason with them by the *sunnah*, because they cannot find any escape from that." (*Nahju 'l-balāghah*, Letter no. 78)

He meant by this that the Qur'ān is concerned with universalities, and in disputation one side will take one thing as its referrent and reason according to that, while another side will take another thing and use that in arguing and disputing; this will naturally give no result. The Khawārij, he wanted to say, did not have enough understanding that they could perceive something true in the Qur'ān and harmonise it with its real applications. Thus he advised Ibn 'Abbās to speak with them following the *sunnah* which is particular, and has pointed out the applications. 'Alī pointed here to the inflexibility and mental ossification in their religiosity which showed their inability to harmonise intellection and religion.

The Khawārij were just a growth of ignorance and stagnation. They had no power to examine and analyse, and they were unable to differentiate between the universal and its application; they imagined that since the arbitration had gone wrong in this instance, its whole foundation must have been null and void, even though there existed the possibility that it would have been well-established and firm, only its application in this instance being incorrect. Thus we see three stages in the story of this arbitration:

i. On historical evidence, 'Alī was not happy to have arbitration; he knew the proposal of Mu'āwiyah's companions to be a trick and a deception. He strongly insisted on this point and refused to be moved.

ii. He said, once it had been decided to form an arbitration council, that Abū Mūsā was a man without foresight and had no competence for the job; a competent man had to be chosen, and he himself recommended Ibn 'Abbās or Mālik al-Ashtar.

iii. The basis of arbitration is correct and is not dangerous. 'Alī also insisted on this point. ⇒

⇐ In *al-Kāmil fi 'l-lughah wa 'l-adab*, the author, Abū 'l-'Abbās al-Mubarrad writes (Egyptian ed., vol. 2, p. 134):

> " 'Alī had personally pleaded with the Khawārij, and had said to them: 'By God, were any of you, like me, against arbitration?'
>
> "'By God,' they replied, 'you are witness that none of us were!'
>
> "'Did you not encourage me,' he said, 'to accept?'
>
> "'By God,' they replied, 'you are witness that we did!'
>
> "'So why,' he continued,'are you against me now, and why have you ostracised me?'
>
> "'We have committed a great sin,' they went on, 'and we must repent. We have repented, and you must repent.'
>
> "Hereupon 'Alī said: '*astaghfiru'llāh min kullī dhanbin* - O God, I ask your forgiveness for every wrong-doing.'
>
> Then these people, who were about six thousand, returned and said that 'Alī had repented and that they were ready for his order to march on Damascus. al-Ash'ath ibn Qays al-Kindī came to 'Alī and said: 'The people say that you recognise arbitration to be an error, and keeping to it to be disbelief in Islam.'
>
> "'Alī went up on the minbar and delivered a speech in which he said: 'Anyone who imagines that I have gone back on the arbitration imagines mistakenly, and anyone who thinks that arbitration is an error is himself in greater error.'
>
> "Then the Khawārij left the mosque and once again rebelled against 'Alī."

'Alī had said that in this case there had been a mistake, in the sense that Mu'āwiyah and his companions had wished to resort to deceit, and in the sense that Abū Mūsā had been inefficient even though 'Alī had from the beginning said that he should not have been chosen. But that was not to be taken to mean that the basis of arbitration was void.

* * * * *

As for any difference between the rule of the Qur'ān and the rule of individual people, no differentiation was made. The acceptance of the rule or governance of the Qur'ān means that in all events what ever the Qur'ān exhorts us to do should be done, whereas the rule or governance of individuals means following the decisions and opinions of these persons. Now, since the Qur'ān cannot speak, its truth must be derived by the implementation of particular applications, and that would be impossible without individual persons. On this matter 'Alī said:

> "We did not name people as arbitrators, but we named the Qur'ān as arbitrator. The Qur'ān is a book, bound, between two covers, and it does not speak. It therefore needs an interpreter. Only men can be such interpreters. When these people invited us to name the Qur'ān as arbitrator between us, we could not let ourselves be the party which turned away from the Book of ⇒

⇐ Allāh, since He has said:

فَإِن تَنَازَعْتُمْ فِي شَيْءٍ فَرُدُّوهُ إِلَى اللهِ وَالرَّسُولِ

And then, if you quarrel about anything, refer it to Allāh and the Prophet. (an-Nisā', 4:59)

"Reference to Allāh means that we should decide according to the Qur'ān, while reference to the Prophet means we should follow his *sunnah*. Now, if arbitration were truly implemented through the Qur'ān, we should be the most rightful of people to receive it (the caliphate); and if the arbitration is through the *sunnah* of the Messenger of Allāh, we should be the first of them to receive it." (*Nahju 'l-balāghah*, Sermon no. 124)

There is a problem here concerning the harmonisation of the beliefs of the Shī'ah and the person of Amīr al-mu'minīn (see the end of sermon no. 2 in *Nahju 'l-balāghah*). Rulership and Imāmate in Islam is by divine designation and according to textual bases (*naṣṣ*), so why did 'Alī submit to the decision of arbitration and afterwards firmly defend it?

We can very well understand the answer to this objection from the preceding words of the Imām, for, as he said, if the consideration and judgement were correctly made through the Qur'ān, no conclusion could be derived apart from his right to the caliphate and the Imāmate, and the *sunnah* of the Prophet gives the same conclusion.

The Influence of Islamic Sects on Each Other:

The study of the lives of the Khawārij is profitable for us in so far as we can understand to what extent they have had an effect in Islamic history, from the aspect of politics, from that of beliefs and disposition, and from the legal or prescriptive aspect.

However much various sects and groups may differ from each other in their slogans and principles, it may sometimes happen that the spirit of one sect will penetrate into another one, and the latter, although it may be an opponent of the first, will absorb its spirit and soul. The nature of man is a thief; sometimes one can find people who, for example, may be Sunnī, but who, in spirit and soul, are Shī'ah, and sometimes the other way round. Sometimes someone is naturally very dogmatic, legalistic and outward, but spiritually he is a Ṣūfī, and *vice versa*. Similarly it is possible that some people are Shī'ah by imitation and by their speech, but spiritually and practically Khārijite. This is both true of individuals, and of communities and nations.

When social groups are associated with eath other, even though each of them try to preserve their beliefs, these will spread from one to the other, just as, for example, ⇒

⇐ "*qam-e zanī*" [striking the head with a sword in order to self-inflict wounds, a practice among the common people, like the following two, associated with processions during the mourning ceremonies in the month of Muḥarram] and the beating of drums and blowing of horns, penetrated Iran from the Orthodox Christians of Caucasia [at one time part of Iran], and since the spirit of the people was receptive to these customs, they spread like wild-fire.

For this reason, the spirit of each sect must be uncovered. Sometimes sects are born from a willingness to see good in certain events or persons to "look upon your brother's deed in the best light"; for example, the Sunnī, who were born of a favourable predisposition towards certain personalities. And some sects may be born from a kind of special perspective and emphasis on the principles of Islam, not from individuals and personalities. And occasionally they will be critical people, like the early Shī'ahs. A sect may be born of an emphasis on the inward spirit and the interpretation of this inwardness, like the Sūfīs, and a sect may be born of an emphasis on bigotry and inflexibility, like the Khawārij.

When we have come to understand the spirit of a sect and its first historical circumstances, we are in a better position to judge what ideas passed from this sect to other sects in subsequent centuries, and who adopted their spirit as well as the slogans and the framework of stock phrases. In this respect, beliefs and ideas are like words when, without there being any intention, they enter from the language of one people into the language of another. For example, after the Muslim conquest of Iran, Arabic words entered the Persian language, and, in the opposite direction, some thousand Persian words entered the Arabic language. There is a similar influence of Turkish on the Arabic and Persian languages; as for example with the Turkish of the time of the Caliph al-Mutawakkil, and the Turkish of the Seljuqs and the Mongols; and it is the same story with the rest of the world's languages. Such examples could easily be extended to fashions and tastes.

The way of thinking and the spirit of the ideas of the Khawārij - the inflexibility of their minds and the disengagement of intellection and religiosity in their thought - have leaked into the Islamic community down through the history of Islam in various forms. However much other sects may have considered themselves opponents of them, we can still see the spirit of the Khārijism in their ways of thinking; and the only reason for this is the result of what we said: the nature of man is a thief, and it is easy to keep company with this thief.

A number of the Khawārij have always believed that their slogans should battle with anything new. They even give a holy aura to the means of life, about which we spoke when we said that no material means or external form has been sanctified in Islam, ⇒

⇐ and they consider the use of every new means as disbelief in Islam and atheism.

Among Islamic schools of beliefs and sciences, and in law too, we see those which were born from the spirit of the disengagement of intellection from religion, and such schools of thought are a perfect example of Khārijite thought. They completely repudiate the use of the intellect in discovering reality and in deriving secondary laws; they call the following of the intellect innovation and ungodliness, even though in many verses the Qur'ān summons man in the direction of his intellect and establishes human insight and understanding as the cornerstone of the Divine call.

The Mu'tazilah, who came into existence at the beginning of the second century of the Hijrah, took their origins in the wake of the discussion of, and investigation into, the interpretation of belief and unbelief, as to whether commission of the larger sins necessarily resulted in the sinner becoming a disbeliever or not; and naturally their coming into existence was connected with the Khārijites. The Mu'tazilah were people who wanted a degree of free thinking, and to create an intellectual life. Although they did not benefit from any kind of scientific basis or origin, they managed to investigate, and think about, Islamic problems, to a certain extent quite freely. They critically evaluated *aḥādīth* to a certain degree, and they only followed those ideas and opinions which had been researched according to their own beliefs.

From the beginning, the Mu'tazilah took a stand against the disputes and opposition from those who based everything on *aḥādīth*, and from the exoterists. These latter, who only recognised the outward meaning of *aḥādīth* as evidence, and who would have nothing to do with the spirit or inner meaning of the Qur'ān and *aḥādīth*, did not believe that any clear judgements could follow from the intellect. However much the Mu'tazilah valued intellectual reflexion, these people considered that value could be attached only to outward meanings.

In the space of the one and a half centuries that passed in the life of this intellectual school of dissent, amazing ups and downs befell them, till, in the end, the Ash'arites came into being, and once again the value of sheer intellectual thinking and reflexion and the reckonings of pure metaphysics were denied. These Ash'arites claimed that it was necessary for Muslims to believe in the exoteric meanings of traditional explanations and not to think or reflect upon their deeper meanings; every kind of question and answer, or why and wherefore, was an innovation for them. Imām Aḥmad ibn Ḥanbal, who was one of the four Imāms of the Sunnīs, was strongly opposed to the way of thinking of the Mu'tazilah, to such an extent that he went to prison for his opinion and was tortured, but he still affirmed his opposition.

In the end, the Ash'arites were the winners, and the school of intellectual thinking ⇒

As a result of their short-sightedness, the Khawārij practically refused to recognise other Muslims as Muslims, refused to recognise the animals

⇐ closed down; and this victory dealt a great blow to the intellectual life of Islamic sciences.

The Ash'arites thought the Mu'tazilah innovators, and one of the Ash'arite poets wrote after their victory:

The reign of the people of innovation has come to an end.
Their yarn has become brittle and has broken;
The party which the Devil formed from them
Have warbled away to each other till they became split up.
O Companions in thought! Did they have a jurist
Or an Imām to lead them in their innovations?

The Akhbārī school was also a kind of dissociation of intellection and religion. They were a Shī'ite school of jurists, and they reached the height of their powers in the eleventh and twelfth centuries of the Hijrah (18th century A.D.). They had a lot in common with the exoteric school and the traditionalists among the Sunnīs. In their way of deriving laws, both schools followed the same method, their only difference being in which *aḥādīth* they chose to follow.

The Akhbārīs completely shut down the work of the intellect, and denied any value or power of proof to the perceptions of the intellect in the derivation of the rulings of Islam from their texts. They considered the following of the intellect to be absolutely forbidden, and in their writings they led a campaign against the Uṣūlīs, who were the followers of the other Shī'ite school of legal thought. They said that the only sources of proof were the Qur'ān and the *sunnah.* Of course, they also said that the power of proof of the Qur'ān was by way of the exegesis given by the *sunnah* and *aḥādīth*; so in fact, they virtually disregarded the Qur'ān as a source of proof and only recognised the outward meaning of ahadith to be trustworthy.

Now we are not planning to go into a discussion of the ways in which various currents of Islamic thought differ from each other, and consider in detail those schools which have adopted the split between intellection and religion, which is what we have called the spirit of Khārijism. This would be a very lengthy discussion. Our only aim was to show what the influences of the sects have been on each other, and that the Khārijite sect, although it did not last long, continued to manifest its spirit in every century and age of Islam up to the present when a number of contemporary writers and "intellectuals" of the Islamic world have produced their way of thinking in a modern and up-to-date form by associating it with empirical philosophy.

they slaughtered as lawful food, recognised the spilling of their blood as lawful and marriage with them as prohibited.

* * * * *

THE POLITICS OF "USING" THE QUR'ĀN

It is now some thirteen centuries that the politics of "holding the Qur'ān upon a spear" has been more or less prevalent among the Muslims. It becomes especially rife among those who wish to profit from it whenever sanctimoniousness and exotericism increases and it becomes fashionable to display one's piety and asceticism. There are two lessons to be learnt from this.

Firstly, whenever the ignorant, the unknowing and the uninformed put on a show of sanctity and piety, and people take them to be the symbol of the practising Muslim, an excellent tool is available for unscrupulous schemers. Such schemers always turn these people into an instrument for their own ends, and make their presence a strong hindrance to the ideas of real reformers. It is quite common to see anti-Islamic elements making quite open use of this means, that is to say, setting the power of Islam itself to work against Islam. Western colonialism has had much experience in the use of this means, and has in its turn profited from deceitful arousal of the sentiments of the Muslims, especially in the field of the creation of schisms between them. What a disgrace it is when, for example, afflicted Muslims plan to drive out foreign influence, and then see the very people they wanted to save turn into a barrier in their path in the name, and under the banner, of religion. Indeed, if the masses of the people are ignorant and uninformed, hypocrites will use the fortress of Islam itself. In Iran, where the people have the honour to love and follow the Household of the Prophet (*Ahlu 'l-bayt*), hypocrites are creating a fortress against the Qur'ān, Islam and the Household of the Prophet to help the usurping Jews, out of the holy fortress of love of the Household of the Prophet, and in their sacred name, and this is the most abominable part of the injustice against Islam, the Qur'ān, the Prophet and his Household. The Prophet said:

إِنِّي مَا أَخَافُ عَلَى أُمَّتِي الفَقْرَ، وَلَكِنْ أَخَافُ عَلَيْهِمْ سُوءَ التَّدْبِيرِ

I am not anxious about the incursion of poverty among my community; that about which I am afraid for them is crooked thinking. That which poverty of thought will bring my community is much worse than that which economic poverty will bring them.

Secondly, we must try to make our methodology of derivation from the Qur'ān a true one. The Qur'ān is a leader and a guide when it is subjected to true reflection, when it is interpreted wisely, when guidance is taken from the people who really know the Qur'ān, who are firmly rooted in the sciences of the Qur'ān. As long as our methodology is wrong, and as long as we do not learn how to benefit from the Qur'ān, we shall not drive any profit from it. Profiteers or ignorant people sometimes read the Qur'ān, and then follow up an incorrect possibility. Just as you have probably heard in the words of *Nahju 'l-balāghah*, "they say the word 'truth', and then set their minds of falsehood!" This is not practicising the Qur'ān or bringing it to life, this is putting it to death. The Qur'ān is put into practice when it is understood with a true understanding.

The Qur'ān always presents its project in a general and fundamental form, but the deduction and harmonisation of the particular to the universal depends on our correct under standing and conceptualisation. For example, we do not find written in the Qur'ān that in a war that took place on a certain day between 'Alī and Mu'āwiyah, 'Alī was in the right; all we find in the Qur'ān is that:

وَإِن طَائِفَتَانِ مِنَ الْمُؤْمِنِينَ اقْتَتَلُوا فَأَصْلِحُوا بَيْنَهُمَا ۖ فَإِن بَغَتْ إِحْدَاهُمَا عَلَى الْأُخْرَىٰ فَقَاتِلُوا الَّتِي تَبْغِي حَتَّىٰ تَفِيءَ إِلَىٰ أَمْرِ اللَّهِ

If two parties of believers fight, put things right between them; then, if one of them is insolent against the other, fight the insolent one till it reverts to Allāh's commandment. (al-Ḥujarāt, 49:9)

This is the Qur'ān and its way of explanation; but it does not say in such-and-such a war so-and-so was in the right and the other was in the wrong.

The Qur'ān does not spell out names; it does not say: after forty years, more or less, a man called Mu'āwiyah will appear who will fight with 'Alī, and you should fight in that war for 'Alī. And neither should it enter into particulars. The Qur'ān's task is not to make a list of subjects and point out which is right and which is wrong; such a thing would be impossible. The Qur'ān came to stay for ever, so it has to make fundamental and universal things clear, so that falsehood can take its place face to face with truth in every age and people can act according to the criterion of these universalities. It is therefore a duty for people to open their eyes to the basic advice: "*if two parties of believers fight. . .*", and distinguish between the party doing the terrorizing and the one that is being terrorized; and to accept if the unruly party ceases to be unruly. But if they stop, and try to be cunning so as to save themselves from defeat, and prepare themselves for a new attack, and become unruly again, and, in the words of the Qur'ān, "*if one of them is insolent against the other*", be firm, and do not give way to their cunning.

It is up to the poeple themselves to discriminate in all these matters. The Qur'ān seeks that the Muslims should be intellectually and socially mature, and a necessary consequence of such intellectual maturity is the ability to differentiate between the just man and the unjust man. The Qur'ān did not come to be always for people like a guardian over a juvenile, to carry out the particular details of their lives like a personal protector, and to specify each special case by a material sign and indicator.

Actually, knowing people, the degree of their competence, the limits to their fitness for, and relationship to, Islam and Islamic realities is itself a duty, and frequently we neglect this duty.

'Alī, may peace be upon him, said:

أَنَّكُمْ لَنْ تَعْرِفُوا الرُّشْدَ حَتَّى تَعْرِفُوا الَّذِي تَرَكَهُ

You will never know truth and follow the right way unless you know the person who has abandoned it.[22]

Knowing the principles and the generalities is alone not enough unless their correspondence and reference to particulars has been found, for it is possible that, through an error of judgement concerning persons and individuals or through ignorance of the situation, one will act in the name of truth and Islam and under the banner of Islam against Islam and truth and for falsehood.

Injustice and the unjust, justice and the just are mentioned in the Qur'ān, but their applications must be sought out. We must not mistake injustice and justice for injustice, and then cut off the head of justice and truth in the name of what we imagine to be a universal principle and thejudgement of the Qur'ān.

* * * * *

THE NECESSITY OF FIGHTING HYPOCRISY

The most difficult struggle is the one against hypocrisy, for it is the struggle against the cunning who use the stupid as their weapon. This fight is several degrees more difficult than the fight with unbelief, because, in the battle with unbelief, the struggle is against an unconcealed, open and unhidden current, while the struggle against hypocrisy is in fact a struggle against concealed unbelief. Hypocrisy has two faces: one is the outward face - Islam and Muslim; the other inward - unbelief and evil. It is very difficult for the ordinary people to spot this latter aspect, and sometimes impossible; and thus the struggle with hypocrisy ends in failure because the great majority of people cannot

22. *Nahju 'l-balāghah*, Sermon no. 146.

extend the reach of their perception beyond outward forms and the hidden does not become apparent. They do not have a long enough range to penetrate the depths of the inward nature of things.

Amīr al-mu'minīn (a.s.) wrote in the letter he sent to Muḥammad ibn Abī Bakr

> The Messenger of Allāh said to me: "I do not fear for my community from the believer or the unbeliever. As the believer, Allāh will protect him because of his belief, and, as for the unbeliever, Allāh will humiliate him because of his unbelief. But I fear about everyone of you who is a hypocrite in his heart and learned in speech. He speaks what you can accept, but he does what you cannot accept.[23]

The Prophet here points out the danger in hypocrisy and the hypocrite, because the majority of people are uninformed and unaware, and are taken in by outward appearances.[24]

---

23. *ibid.*, Letter no. 27.

24. Thus we see throughout the history of Islam that every time a reformer arises on behalf of the people to reform the state of their society and religion, and the interests of the unjust and the profiteers are endangered, these latter immediately don the disguise of sanctity, and display their piety and religion.

When al-Ma'mūn ar-Rashīd, the 'Abbāssid Caliph famous in the history of rulers for his epicurianism and extravagance, saw that the 'Alawīs were on the ascendence, he put on a change of clothing and showed himself in public in a new light. Then Abū Ḥānifah al-Iskāfī, who neither took a penny from him, nor benefited from him, praised him for this and composed the following panegyric:

O Ma'mūn, the like of whom among the rulers of the State of Islam
Has never been seen, by Arab or by simple peasant,
Wore a coat of fur for so long
That it became old, worn and tatty.
His close companions were amazed at this excess
And asked him for the reason for this.
He said. "Tales are left behind by kings
Among the Arabs and the non-Arabs, not by fine cotton and linen!"

And so on, each in his way excelling in the well-tried and oppressive politics of ⇒

Care must be taken over the fact that with every bit that stupidity increases, the way opens further for hypocrisy. The struggle with the stupid and stupidity is the struggle with hypocrisy too, for the stupid are the tool in the hands of the hypocrites. Naturally, the struggle with the foolish and with foolishness is to disarm the hypocrites, and take the sword out of their hands.

* * * * *

'ALĪ, THE TRUE IMĀM AND LEADER

In all aspects of 'Alī's existence, of his history and biography, of his dispositions and habits, of his character and behaviour, of his words and speech, there is instruction, examples to follow, teaching and leadership. Just as 'Alī's "power of attraction" taught us and instructed us, so also

⇐ "holding the Qur'ān up on spears", and defeating all effort and self-sacrifice, nipping each new resurgence in the bud. This is nothing but the ignorance and unknowing of people, which does not know how to distinguish between slogans and reality, thus closing the way of resurgence and reformation to themselves, and then realising that all the preparatory work has been cancelled out and that they must start at the beginning again.

Of all the great points we learn from the life of 'Alī, we see that this kind of struggle is not confined to any special group, but that everywhere that a group of Muslims, or those who are got up in the garb of religion, become a tool for the advance of non-Muslims and the progress of colonialism, and the colonialists, for the protection of their own interests, give them cover, and then use them as their shield, so that it becomes impossible to fight them without doing away with the shields, then it is necessary to begin by fighting with these shields and destroying them so as to remove the obstacle in the way and be able to attack at the heart of the enemy. Perhaps the machinations of Mu'āwiyah had something to do with the Khawārij's sabotage, and therefore even on that day Mu'āwiyah, or at least people like al-Ash'ath ibn al-Qays, and other elements in the sabotage and disturbances, gave cover to the Khawārij.

The history of the Khawārij teaches us the fact that in every resurgence the "shields" must first be got rid of and the fools fought with, just as 'Alī, after the events of the arbitration, first of all attacked the Khawārij and then intended to follow upon the tracks of Mu'āwiyah.

does his "power of repelling". Usually in *ziyārat*[25] to 'Alī and the other Pure Ones we claim we are "the friend of your friend and the enemey of your enemy".

Another way of putting this would be to say: "We will go towards that point which is in the lines of force of attraction to you and which you attract, and we will choose to be far from that point which you repulse."

What we have said in this book is an intimation of 'Alī's powers of "attraction and repulsion", and our brevity is particularly apparent in the case of his "repulsion". However, it is clear from what we said that 'Alī strongly repelled two groups - artful hypocrites, and stupid ascetics.

These two lessons are sufficient for those who claim to be his "party" - the Shī'ahs - to open their eyes and not be duped by hypocrites, to keep their vision acute and dismiss the outward aspect of things, two things with which the Shī'ah community is now sorely afflicted.

* * * * *

25. A kind of supplication addressed to one or all of the fourteen *ma'ṣūm* (immaculates) - the Prophet, his daughter Fatimah, and the twelve Imams. (tr.)